# This Journal Belongs To:

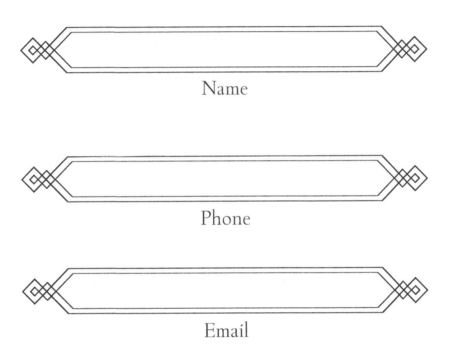

Name

Phone

Email

IF YOU FIND THIS JOURNAL
PLEASE CONTACT ME

## The lives of people around the globe have been radically changed from using this guide and reading the Bible cover to cover!

"I have been a Christian my whole life, but I had never read the Bible cover to cover. Reading it starting from the beginning has given me a broader perspective of God's full picture and that He had a plan from the beginning to the end of time. He has always been faithful. Knowing that He has a plan has given me the freedom to step into the unique purpose He has for me in life. Get busy, get moving, and get in the Word and see what God has for you!" ~Christina Stempke, CA

"I have been reading the Bible for 58 years. I have started to read the Bible cover to cover so many times and never successfully finished it. Doing it in a group and having journal questions has allowed me the chance to finally get through all of the Bible. It helped me to dive deep. I never realized how much the Bible, old and new, go together. It has built my faith so strong through this whole process. I plan on doing it every year!" ~Karen Sanchez Wright, CA

"I love the Word just soaking through me. I listen to it mainly as I commute to and from my son's house to watch my grandchildren. I just let the Holy Spirit feed me. ~Julie Bowen Stern, FL

"Spending time with Him in His word has made me hungry for more and has grounded me. Plus, it has given me new understanding because He gives us the sight to "see" what He desires to reveal. Every season is different and it's beautiful how fresh the Word is every day. I had no idea how much I loved the Old Testament. Reading it today feels so relevant, and the joy of integration for meaning today created such light. His timing is perfect. I've found myself less self-reliant, and trusting God in faith this year reading the Bible consistently. My relationship with him is so much deeper, which pours out into my other relationships." ~Janet Johnson, SC

"My understanding of scripture has deepened. My relationship with God grows every day. I am more aware to offer mercy and grace to others. I am so thankful for this Bible study and the group I have been able to read the Bible with. I am sad to think about when it's over." ~María López, PA

"I have always wanted to read the Bible from beginning to end. The more I seek his Word the more I want to know and understand. I will be starting over again to see what I get out of it the second time around. Surprisingly, my husband wants to listen to it the next round. I think he sees how much I have grown in my search for God's word that he is feeling left out!" ~Deb Gerken Thompson, ND

"I have loved reading the scriptures! Love the restoration of the name in the Word and learning some Hebrew as well! His faithfulness has been amazing. Family relationships have been restored and so much more!" ~Sonja Lee, WI

"I have found so much goodness reading the Bible cover to cover. I love the Gospels! I have loved creating a habit of reading the Word and greater intimacy with the Father." ~Savannah Dyer, CA

"This Bible challenge has been amazing because the Bible has come alive in a whole new way for me! Even when I have gotten behind on my weekly reading, God has spoken to me so powerfully. Even in scriptures I previously thought were dull and boring, God spoke to me exactly what I needed to hear in that moment of my life. You are never really behind; God's timing is perfect. Just keep pressing forward."
~Jeanmarie Kaehler, WA

"My Bishop's wife first told me to start reading with the book of Psalms and later gave me other books to read, but never in order. This is the first time I have gone through the Bible like this. This study has revealed the Bible to me in a new and deeper way. I can see how everything is repeated at least once, and how the Old Testament and New Testament back each other up. And I am now seeing God's love throughout the Bible more than I ever have before." ~Sharilyn Garrett, MI

"This is my first time reading through the entire Bible. I have been blown away by so much! There is no new evil under the sun. God's mercy is great for His people. I have gained a new awe at what Jesus did for us in light of what God's people had to do before Jesus. I am so grateful for each daily reader! It definitely helped me stay on track. Thank you, Summer, for inviting us on this incredible journey!!" ~Naomi Glick, PA

"I have learned so much about God, and what He wants from us. I feel like I'm learning everyday who He is, and how much He loves us. It truly feels like I am gaining a deeper relationship with him. It's all wisdom!"
~Marissa Cooper, TX

"I have read through the Bible twice, but I did it on my own. Having 6,000 women doing it with me has been wonderful. God has blessed me with several women who are encouraging me to step out in faith and share prayer requests more instead of bottling everything up. I am praying a lot more and crying out to God." ~Fran Toal, United Kingdom

"I have always struggled with being consistent in reading God's Word. And to be honest, at the beginning, I struggled to keep up. I did a lot of praying those first few weeks. But since getting on track, this truly has helped me. I feel closer to Jesus. God has taught me through this to love myself and to know I am his daughter. But most importantly, to also listen to Him. Thank you, Summer, for this group. It also has given me over 6,000 new sisters too!" ~Kristy Gannaway, AL

"My life has changed a lot since I started reading the Bible cover to cover. I am at a loss for words, or how to even describe it. I am so proud of myself that I have kept up with the reading. It has opened up my heart. I have more of an understanding of God's Word and a much closer relationship with Him. It's like I am in a whole new world now, and even though there is bad stuff going on in the world, I no longer worry because I know God has got me!" ~Tina Mader, MI

"Reading the Bible cover to cover in a year has kept me accountable. It has been challenging, but very rewarding, to also lead a group of 10 women through it as well. Sometimes the women would get behind, but they would not give up and then would find the time to catch up. I am grateful that they helped keep me accountable, too! This year has pushed me to dig and want to know Him more. Many times, over and over, He has shown up and told me not to fear but to have faith because He will take care of things."
~Edith Schmidt, Canada

—⋈ SECOND EDITION ⋈—

# A YEAR OF MIRACLES

## 52 WEEK BIBLE STUDY JOURNAL

A guide to reading the Bible cover to cover in a year

Copyright © 2023 Fear Into Faith Incorporated

All rights reserved. No part of this publication may be reproduced, distributed, or transmitted in any form or by any means, including photocopying, recording, or other electronic methods, without the prior written permission from the publisher, except in the case of brief quotations embodied in critical reviews and certain other noncommercial uses permitted by copyright law. Requests to the publisher for permission should be addressed to the Permissions Department, Fear Into Faith, 8553 N. Beach St. PMB# 152, Fort Worth, TX 76244

LIMIT OF LIABILITY/ DISCLAIMER OF WARRANTY: The information in each non-fiction book is intended for use within the United States of America. Each book is meant as a general resource book; it is not meant to provide any legal advice. The Publisher and the Author make no representations or warranties with respect to the accuracy or completeness of the contents of the work and specifically disclaim all warranties of fitness for a particular purpose. The advice and strategies contained therein may not be suitable for every situation. The work is sold with the understanding that the Publisher and the Author are not providing any legal, accounting, or other professional services. If legal, accounting, or other expert assistance is required, the services of competent professionals should be sought. Neither the publisher nor the author shall be liable for damages arising herefrom. The fact that an organization or website is referred to in this work as a citation and/or a potential source of further information does not mean that the author or the publisher endorses the information the organization or website may provide or recommendations it may make. Further, readers should be aware that Internet websites listed in this work may have changed or disappeared between when this work was written and when it is read. The information contained is strictly for educational purposes. Therefore, if you wish to apply ideas contained in this book, or related publications, products, and programs, you are taking full responsibility for your actions. By using this product, you agree that the Publisher and the author cannot be held responsible – directly or indirectly, in full or in part – for any damages or losses that may be suffered as a result of taking action on the information published in this book.

First paperback edition September 2023

Interior Design: Jeremy Holden
Cover Design: Sharon Marta
Editors: Christine Coe, Sandi Jenkins & Allison Johnson
ISBN: Print 978-1-7374648-5-3

"Scripture quotations are from The ESV® Bible (The Holy Bible, English Standard Version®), copyright © 2001 by Crossway, a publishing ministry of Good News Publishers. Used by permission. All rights reserved."

Published in the United States of America

Ordering Information:

Quantity sales - Special discounts are available on quantity purchases by churches, corporations, associations, U.S. trade bookstores, wholesalers, and others. For details, contact the publisher at Press@FearIntoFaith.com.

**For Free Resources and Videos on "How to Use this Bible Study Journal" scan this QR code to download our app.**

The author has made every effort to ensure the accuracy of the information within this book was correct and true at the time of publication. The stories printed are the personal accounts of those that submitted them, and not of the author. The author does not assume and hereby disclaims any liability to any party for any loss, damage, or disruption caused by errors or omissions, whether such errors or omissions result from accident, negligence, or any other cause.

This book is dedicated to my "bestie of all time," Christina Stempke. Thank you for your decades of friendship, your never-ending love & support, and for holding my arms up each time God asked me to stretch them higher. I love you more than words can express. None of this would be possible without you.

## Contents

A Note From The Journal Creator . . . . . . . . . . . . . . . . . . . . . . . . . . . . . . . . . . XI
What You Will Find In This Journal . . . . . . . . . . . . . . . . . . . . . . . . . . . . . . . XII
Your Journey Begins Here! . . . . . . . . . . . . . . . . . . . . . . . . . . . . . . . . . . . . XIV
What Can God Not Do? . . . . . . . . . . . . . . . . . . . . . . . . . . . . . . . . . . . . . . XVI

| | | | | | |
|---|---|---|---|---|---|
| Week 1 . . . . . . . . . . . . . . | 17 | Week 19 . . . . . . . . . . . . | 89 | Week 37 . . . . . . . . . . . | 161 |
| Week 2 . . . . . . . . . . . . . . | 21 | Week 20 . . . . . . . . . . . . | 93 | Week 38 . . . . . . . . . . . | 165 |
| Week 3 . . . . . . . . . . . . . . | 25 | Week 21 . . . . . . . . . . . . | 97 | Week 39 . . . . . . . . . . . | 169 |
| Week 4 . . . . . . . . . . . . . . | 29 | Week 22 . . . . . . . . . . . . | 101 | Week 40 . . . . . . . . . . . | 173 |
| Week 5 . . . . . . . . . . . . . . | 33 | Week 23 . . . . . . . . . . . . | 105 | Week 41 . . . . . . . . . . . | 177 |
| Week 6 . . . . . . . . . . . . . . | 37 | Week 24 . . . . . . . . . . . . | 109 | Week 42 . . . . . . . . . . . | 181 |
| Week 7 . . . . . . . . . . . . . . | 41 | Week 25 . . . . . . . . . . . . | 113 | Week 43 . . . . . . . . . . . | 185 |
| Week 8 . . . . . . . . . . . . . . | 45 | Week 26 . . . . . . . . . . . . | 117 | Week 44 . . . . . . . . . . . | 189 |
| Week 9 . . . . . . . . . . . . . . | 49 | Week 27 . . . . . . . . . . . . | 121 | Week 45 . . . . . . . . . . . | 193 |
| Week 10 . . . . . . . . . . . . . | 53 | Week 28 . . . . . . . . . . . . | 125 | Week 46 . . . . . . . . . . . | 197 |
| Week 11 . . . . . . . . . . . . . | 57 | Week 29 . . . . . . . . . . . . | 129 | Week 47 . . . . . . . . . . . | 201 |
| Week 12 . . . . . . . . . . . . . | 61 | Week 30 . . . . . . . . . . . . | 133 | Week 48 . . . . . . . . . . . | 205 |
| Week 13 . . . . . . . . . . . . . | 65 | Week 31 . . . . . . . . . . . . | 137 | Week 49 . . . . . . . . . . . | 209 |
| Week 14 . . . . . . . . . . . . . | 69 | Week 32 . . . . . . . . . . . . | 141 | Week 50 . . . . . . . . . . . | 213 |
| Week 15 . . . . . . . . . . . . . | 73 | Week 33 . . . . . . . . . . . . | 145 | Week 51 . . . . . . . . . . . | 217 |
| Week 16 . . . . . . . . . . . . . | 77 | Week 34 . . . . . . . . . . . . | 149 | Week 52 . . . . . . . . . . . | 221 |
| Week 17 . . . . . . . . . . . . . | 81 | Week 35 . . . . . . . . . . . . | 153 | Walk In His Ways . . . . . | 225 |
| Week 18 . . . . . . . . . . . . . | 85 | Week 36 . . . . . . . . . . . . | 157 | | |

Prayer Log . . . . . . . . . . . . . . . . . . . . . . . . . . . . . . . . . . . . . . . . . . . . . . . . 226
Praise Report . . . . . . . . . . . . . . . . . . . . . . . . . . . . . . . . . . . . . . . . . . . . . 228
Save The Date! . . . . . . . . . . . . . . . . . . . . . . . . . . . . . . . . . . . . . . . . . . . . 232
Free Gift . . . . . . . . . . . . . . . . . . . . . . . . . . . . . . . . . . . . . . . . . . . . . . . . 235
About The Journal Creator . . . . . . . . . . . . . . . . . . . . . . . . . . . . . . . . . . . 236
Pastoral & Biblical Advisor . . . . . . . . . . . . . . . . . . . . . . . . . . . . . . . . . . . 236

# A Note from the Journal Creator

In April 2020, I finished reading the Bible cover to cover for the first time. My goal was to finish it in one year, it took me two. When I finished, I felt God telling me to do it again and this time to hit my goal.

So... I did a Facebook Live to see if anyone would want to read the Bible with me in a year and hold me accountable. I was hoping to find five friends to read with me. Before I finished that Facebook Live, I had more than 20 women wanting to read the Bible with me. To my surprise, those women began to share my video with their friends and by the end of that day we had over 200 women join. Then, in the days to come, it jumped to 1,000, then 2,000, and then 4,000!

On July 13, 2020 we started the "Fear Into Faith 52-Week Bible Challenge" with over 6,700 women. And to be honest with you - I was freaked out! I cried out to God on my bathroom floor and told Him all the reasons why I was not qualified to lead thousands of women through reading the Bible. God was so gentle with me at that moment. He told me that He had made me a "gatherer of people and a natural encourager," and all He wanted was for me to encourage as many women as possible to read His word cover to cover and He would qualify me for all the rest.

I had no idea how to pull something like this off. A friend suggested that we use a women's Bible Study she had been using. It had a weekly reading plan and journal questions - it was perfect! Until it suddenly jumped to Matthew. Oh no! Women were now confused. "Do we jump ahead to the New Testament now?" "What do we do?" they asked. God was very clear to me that He wanted us to read the Bible cover to cover, like we read every other book. I told the women that we would no longer use that guide and we would find something else. We searched high and low and could not find a Bible study that went through the Bible cover to cover. It didn't exist!

So, we created it.

Here we are, years later, with our fourth Bible Study Journal in your hands. We have men and children doing this Bible study now, and we also have a much bigger vision from God than we ever imagined! Our mission now is to lead one million people to read the Bible cover to cover in a year. And...crazily enough...I am no longer freaked out!

I have seen incredible fruits in my own life from being in God's Word each and every day, and from truly surrendering my life to Him. I want to see God's people be fierce for His Kingdom. And that happens through prayer and reading His Word. Reading God's Word from Genesis to Revelations changed my life. I know it will change yours. I will be praying for you to stick with it and finish, my friend. I promise you it's worth it!

Blessings,

*Summer Dey*

# Your Journey Begins Here!

## What materials do you need:

- ☐ This journal
- ☐ Any version or translation of the Bible you would like to use
- ☐ A pen
- ☐ Bible highlighters

*\*We recommend you do not use regular highlighters on your Bible as they can bleed through and destroy pages.*

## How to use this guide:

Here are some tips to help you use this guide and to succeed in your journey:

- **Begin when you want.** You can start this journal whenever it works best for you. We will be launching our yearly Bible Challenge on September 18, 2023. If you'd like to join others from around the world and read along with them then you will want to start then.

- **Find a friend to read with you or lead a group.** There is nothing like accountability to help you achieve your goals. Using this guide and reading the Bible with a friend or a group of people will dramatically increase your chances of finishing reading the Bible in the next year. Plus, you'll play a role in helping others to strengthen their relationship with the Lord as well.

- **Give yourself grace.** Nearly everyone falls behind at some point. The trick is to catch back up as soon as you can and not give up. If you get too far behind you can choose to jump to where you should be in the reading schedule and catch up later when you can.

## We Want You to Succeed!

Visit our website **www.BibleRevival.TV** and download our app to access free videos and resources to go along with this journal.

- Tips on how to highlight your Bible
- Details on how to use each section of this journal
- Frequently asked questions
- How to choose the version of the Bible that's right for you
- And more!

## JOIN OUR COMMUNITY AND EXPERIENCE READING THE BIBLE WITH OTHERS FROM AROUND THE GLOBE!

Your success is important to us! We want to support you with your goal of reading the Bible cover to cover in a year. By purchasing this study guide you have joined people from around the globe, committed to reading God's Word cover to cover in a year, spending more time with Him than ever before, and supporting others to do so as well.

**Join us at www.BibleRevival.TV**

Here's what you get:

- **TV Show** - Our daily Bible TV show *Fear Into Faith - Global Bible Revival* launched in 2023. You can tune in and see the reading assignments read each day. The show features over 100+ different readers and is streamed 6 days a week, and available On-Demand. (Check out the app for more details at *www.BibleRevival.TV*)
- **App** - Our app will put the daily readings right into the palm of your hand and is also a great tool to track your daily reading progress.
- **Email List** - Subscribe to our email list to hear about new book releases, tools, and upcoming resources.
- **Community** - We restart the yearly Bible Challenge every September with people from all over the world. If you join us after that date, you can hop in and jump to whatever chapter we are in. We will be happy to have you!

---

### STOP RIGHT NOW AND SAVE THE DATE!

*September 11-13, 2025, Dallas, TX.*

*END OF THE YEAR CELEBRATION* - We want to celebrate with you when you finish reading the Bible cover to cover. What a HUGE accomplishment! In 2025, we will celebrate on September 11-13th. During this live event you will get the opportunity to finish reading the last few chapters of the book of Revelation out loud together. It is going to be powerful! We would love to have you there! SAVE THE DATE now and plan to join us either live and in-person or virtually online.

# What You Will Find In This Journal

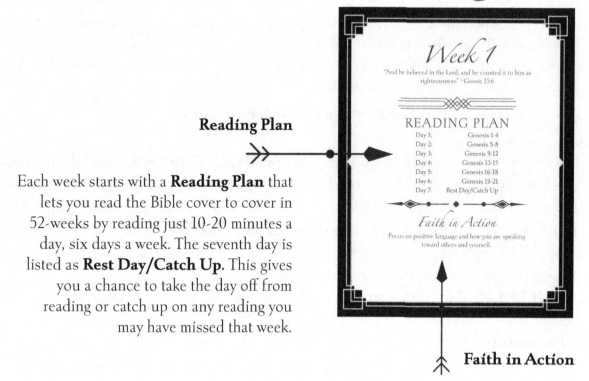

**Reading Plan**

Each week starts with a **Reading Plan** that lets you read the Bible cover to cover in 52-weeks by reading just 10-20 minutes a day, six days a week. The seventh day is listed as **Rest Day/Catch Up**. This gives you a chance to take the day off from reading or catch up on any reading you may have missed that week.

**Faith in Action**

This section has a weekly challenge designed to activate your faith and to take things to a deeper level with the Lord.

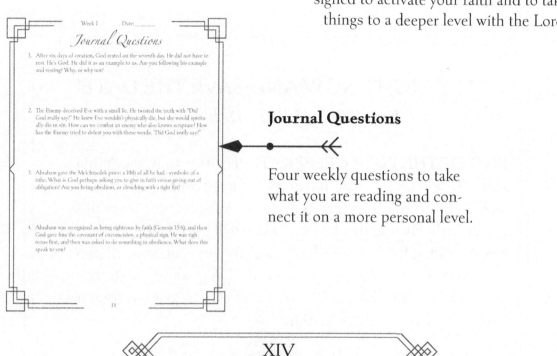

**Journal Questions**

Four weekly questions to take what you are reading and connect it on a more personal level.

### Reflection & Notes

Use this section each week to make note of any questions you had while reading or anything that stands out to you that needs further reflection.

### Gratitude

Use this section to focus on what you are grateful for. What you feed will flourish. When you spend time in gratitude you are shining a light on darkness and it cannot stay. Spend more time in gratitude this year and watch how God shows up!

In the back of the book you will find a **Prayer Log** to track your prayers and see how God answers them.

There is also a **Praise Report** to write down the blessings that God brings into your life.

# What Can God Not Do?

Before you begin this year-long journey...

Imagine for a second what your life will look like a year from now when you have finished reading the Bible cover to cover.

What will your life look like when you have spent that much time with God?

How will it affect you?

How will it affect those around you?

Write out how you visualize your life will be when you finish this incredible goal.

*The vision I have for my life in a year:*

# Week 1

"And he believed in the Lord, and he counted it to him as righteousness." ~*Genesis 15:6*

## READING PLAN

| | |
|---|---|
| Day 1: | Genesis 1-3 |
| Day 2: | Genesis 4-7 |
| Day 3: | Genesis 8-11 |
| Day 4: | Genesis 12-15 |
| Day 5: | Genesis 16-19 |
| Day 6: | Genesis 20-23 |
| Day 7: | Rest Day/Catch Up |

## Faith in Action

Focus on positive language and how you are speaking toward others and yourself.

Week 1    Date: _____

# Journal Questions

1. After six days of creation, God rested on the seventh day. He did not have to rest. He's God. He did it as an example to us. Are you following his example and resting? Why, or why not?

2. The Enemy deceived Eve with a small lie. He twisted the truth with "Did God really say?" How can we combat an enemy who also knows scripture? How has the Enemy tried to defeat you with those words, "Did God really say?"

3. Abraham gave the Melchizedek the priest a tenth of all he had. What is God perhaps asking you to give in faith versus giving out of obligation? Are you being obedient or clenching with a tight fist?

4. Abraham was recognized as being righteous by faith (Genesis 15:6) and then God gave him the covenant of circumcision as a physical sign. He was made righteous first, and then was asked to do something in obedience. What does this speak to you?

## Week 1
## Reflection & Notes

## Gratitude

# Inspiration

I have been in the business of serving God for 37 years as a bishop of a large organization called Prayer Palace Christian Center located in Kampala, Uganda. I oversee 375 satellite churches, a radio station, Dunamis, and recently the government granted me a license for television. I also run an AIDS orphanage which serves children of single parent homes.

The church in Uganda is growing rapidly. Our young men have turned back to God and there is a revival which started in our church in 1995 and its flames still burn today. We believe that if we continue to spread the word of God, we will have turned the nation upside down for Him so that every knee will bow down in Uganda. There is hope, enthusiasm, faith and miracle upon miracle.

In the 1990s, Uganda had the highest rate of AIDS in the world with 40% of the nation infected. It was one of the things that caused our nation to cry out to God. He answered, "If my people, which are called by my name, shall humble themselves, and pray, and seek my face, and turn from their wicked ways; then will I hear from heaven, and will forgive their sin, and will heal their land."

We fasted for 40 days with no results. Another 40 days of fasting yielded nothing. We continued pressing forward and into God for another 40 days - still nothing. We were almost discouraged but a prophetess said that we had been looking to men for help, "now draw your eyes from men, God is about to break out." We took another 40 days, 600 men crying out to God day and night in prayer and in the Word. After 160 days, He instructed us to go into the city where we left prayer cards and posters on every wall that read "The cure for AIDS is in the blood of Jesus."

We left the four walls of the church and went out into a field to preach. Prayers were offered for a woman with AIDS who gave her heart to the Lord. She was instantly healed. When she went back to get her blood drawn they could not find the virus. They drew her blood again and she still tested negative! She came back celebrating and the media flocked to see her. That was the beginning of the miraculous move of God in Uganda.

God exploded as we witnessed many healings, saw tumors disappear, and witch doctors come to Jesus. The crowd grew bigger each day and national revival broke out. A crusade that was supposed to be 14 days lasted five months and grew to over 120,000 people. It would start at 4pm and continue until 4 AM. Every street was packed with traffic jams. Ambulances brought patients to us instead of taking them to the hospital.

By the time we finished this crusade, over 500 people were miraculously healed and medically documented free from AIDS. Doctors flew in from Orange County, CA to verify the machines we use to detect the virus and were shocked to find the very same machines used in the U.S. Some of those doctors got saved right there and then. You could not be in that anointing and fail to receive Jesus.

God has brought us this far to bring us to America to speak into the lives of Americans not to lose hope. There is hope but the church needs to get back on their knees and seek Him. There is still hope for America because God does not forget His remnant. He calls them back into His presence. If the church steps out and begins to cry out, He will break out. We are the fruit of your forefathers. The God you introduced to us is real and He will neither forsake you nor leave you.

*~Bishop Musisi Grivas*

# Week 2

"And she conceived again and bore a son, and said, "This time I will praise the Lord." Therefore she called his name Judah."
~*Genesis 29:35*

## READING PLAN

| | |
|---|---|
| Day 1: | Genesis 24-26 |
| Day 2: | Genesis 27-29 |
| Day 3: | Genesis 30-32 |
| Day 4: | Genesis 33-36 |
| Day 5: | Genesis 37-40 |
| Day 6: | Genesis 41-43 |
| Day 7: | Rest Day/Catch Up |

## Faith in Action

Write out three goals you would like to accomplish over the next year. Be as specific as you can.

Week 2  Date: _____

## Journal Questions

1. God asked Abraham to offer his son, Isaac, as a sacrifice. Abraham obeyed and walked in faith even though God had promised him descendants through Isaac. How can this encourage you in your faith?

2. Esau gave up his birthright for food. His flesh overtook him and he was willing to give up his inheritance. Our inheritance is eternal. Is there hidden sin in your life, or areas you are giving in to the flesh, that can rob you of your inheritance? Are you ready to give them up?

3. Jacob wrestled with God and walked away with a limp. This limp was a physical reminder of humility before God. Are there things in your life that God has used to keep you walking in humility before Him? Pray about this.

4. Joseph was sold into slavery by his own family. After many years God prospered him and placed him in position to bless this same family. What lesson can you personally take from this?

# Week 2
## Reflection & Notes

## Gratitude

# Inspiration

The family was so excited! It was September, 1990, and we were going to have our ultrasound to find out the gender of the first baby on both sides of the family. It wasn't long before we were called back to the ultrasound room. The technician wasn't very chatty, and she didn't even ask us if we wanted to know the baby's gender. She excused herself and came back with the doctor I was scheduled to see that day. He looked somber and said, "I hate to have to give you bad news, but your baby has a choroid plexus cyst. The outcome won't be good. I recommend terminating the pregnancy." The happiest day of our lives took a nosedive.

When I could finally speak, I told the doctor my baby was going to be fine. God was going to heal my baby. Although I had two questions for him. I wanted to know if we were going to have a girl or a boy, and what was a choroid plexus cyst? We were expecting a girl, and a choroid plexus cyst was a cyst that forms in the choroid plexus area of the brain. I worked at one of the largest facilities for the developmentally disabled and special needs population in the South, so knowing what kind of cyst this was interested me. That way I could give all the glory to God for this coming miracle.

The enemy tried to make me afraid, but the love I had for my baby, not to mention my faith in God as my Jehovah Rapha, wouldn't allow me to succumb to fear. After telling us how bad the situation was, the doctor agreed to do a repeat ultrasound in one month. If the cyst had not shrunk or had grown, the pregnancy would be terminated according to him. I told him we'd see him in a month, but God would heal my baby girl!

We got home, and I had my mother and mother-in-law start a prayer chain at their churches. I asked every Christian I knew to pray. God had given me peace that surpassed all understanding. A week before the repeat ultrasound, it happened! I was at a stop sign having just left work, singing the old hymn, "Living By Faith," and knew at that exact moment my baby's brain was healed. It felt as if someone reached into my belly and plucked the cyst out. Well, He did! I couldn't wait to get home to call and tell everyone my news!

The next doctor's appointment finally came. I walked in grinning from ear to ear. I told the ultrasound technician she wouldn't find a cyst because it was gone. She nodded politely. Halfway through the exam, she excused herself. My husband grabbed my hand, not knowing what to think. This time, she came back with several doctors and nurses. The room began to fill up with on-lookers. Many of them were crying. The doctor who suggested terminating my pregnancy told us the cyst was gone. The surrounding brain tissue must have absorbed it. I told him, "Yes, it's gone, but God took it. I felt it when He did." At that, even he had tears glistening in his eyes.

At 6:19 am, on April 18, 1991, my daughter, Blair, was born. She was beautiful and very alert. She still is.

Psalm 139:13-14 states, *"For You created my inmost being; You knitted me together in my mother's womb. I praise You because I am fearfully and wonderfully made; Your works are wonderful; I know full well."* He is a wonder working God!

~Jamie Gatchell

# Week 3

*"The Lord will fight for you, and you have only to be silent."*
*~Exodus 14:14*

## READING PLAN

| | |
|---:|---:|
| Day 1: | Genesis 44-47 |
| Day 2: | Genesis 48-50 |
| Day 3: | Exodus 1-3 |
| Day 4: | Exodus 4-7 |
| Day 5: | Exodus 8-11 |
| Day 6: | Exodus 12-14 |
| Day 7: | Rest Day/Catch Up |

## Faith in Action

Write down three things each day that you are grateful for.

Week 3     Date: _____

# Journal Questions

1. God heard the groaning of His people. Look up the several Hebrew words for "groan" and "cry" in Exodus 2:23-25, to gain a deeper understanding of what this means. Write what you find below. Just like a parent knows their child's cry - God knows yours. Will you trust Him?

2. List the ten plagues that God brought on Egypt. Do you know what these 10 plagues represented and why they were significant?

3. The blood on the doorpost from the Passover lamb was how the Israelites were saved. This was prophetic of Christ as our Passover lamb. What is the significance of applying it to the doorpost? How does this relate to our lives today?

4. God led the Israelites with a cloud by day and fire by night. What might this be symbolic of?

## Week 3
## Reflection & Notes

## Gratitude

# Inspiration

We were at a basketball game when our ten month old daughter, Anthem Bliss, grew lethargic and lost control of her neck. At dinner we noticed she was going downhill and had no facial expressions, so my wife Karissa took her to the ER. By the time I got there, Anthem had a neck brace and IVs coming out of her arms. She was transferred to PICU where she would be for the next couple weeks.

On the second day, Anthem's body went limp and she blacked out. Karissa came behind me, laid her face on the back of my shirt and wept, "Mandrae, tell me this is not how this ends."

This was a moment for me where standing in the gap had never been more real. I was literally between a lifeless baby and a faithless wife. I turned around, grabbed her by both shoulders and said, "We are people of faith. We have to walk by it. We practice faith in the off season, now it is game time. Go home and spend time with God."

They took Anthem for an MRI and I fell on my knees and asked God to move. "I'm not leaving until you bless me." I heard His answer. "Mandrae, I love her more than you will ever love her. Everything will be fine. It's a process and you just have to walk through it."

I dried my eyes and found my wife. I was on fire. I told her God's promise and added, "From this point on, every room she's in will be a room of faith. If you don't have faith, including you as her mother, you're not allowed in there. We have to operate in faith as parents to help connect her hands to the God that never changes and can change everything." Karissa understood and went home to be with the kids and the Lord.

I rested in the hope that I had in Him and what He was able to do because it was beyond my reach. The possible extends to the ends of my fingertips, but the impossible extends beyond that, where God operates.

I walked the hallways of the PICU at midnight praying over babies that maybe didn't have parents praying for them. I knew why we were there. He calls us on the mission field out of comfort to complete His mission. The hospital was a battlefield where He needed His people in position to fight for the rest of His people.

I spoke up in a meeting with doctors, "I've been here for three days now, and everyone seems to have some sort of opinion, but has anyone asked God? The reason I ask is that every day that someone steps foot in my daughter's room, I pray that God guides their hands and their feet before they touch my daughter. Because you can come in there with your own agenda, but God will interrupt your plans because He is in charge of your hands and your thoughts." My hope was that they would question how they handle future patients, especially those in a state of unknown and uncertainty.

It changed the tone because they stood back as we worshiped and prayed over Anthem and doctors would come to us and ask, "What is God saying to you?"

Anthem had a UTI which turned septic. However, I praised God for His protection and told Karissa, "We carried her in, but she's walking out." Two weeks later, she did. She walked out. This event was a testimony to how faith tested produces growth. It taught me what it looks like to stand in the gap, not only for my own family, but for other people too.

~Mandrae Collins

# Week 4

"You are to speak to the people of Israel and say, 'Above all you shall keep My Sabbaths, for this is a sign between Me and you throughout your generations, that you may know that I, the Lord, sanctify you.'" ~*Exodus 31:13*

## READING PLAN

| | |
|---|---|
| Day 1: | Exodus 15-18 |
| Day 2: | Exodus 19-21 |
| Day 3: | Exodus 22-25 |
| Day 4: | Exodus 26-28 |
| Day 5: | Exodus 29-32 |
| Day 6: | Exodus 33-36 |
| Day 7: | Rest Day/Catch Up |

## Faith in Action

Pray for someone who you know is going through a difficult season.

Week 4   Date: _____

# Journal Questions

1. God brought the children of Israel out of bondage and then gave them the Commandments to obey. This is a picture of grace, and how we don't have to do anything but simply believe Him for our salvation. What can we learn from this regarding our own salvation and obedience?

2. The altar they made was of bronze. When the people pushed their sacrifice up on the altar they could likely see their reflection in the altar. How powerful is that? What do you think was the purpose of seeing their own reflection while lifting their animal up to be slain?

3. In Exodus 32, God threatens to destroy the people because of their disobedience. Then, in a marvelous picture of intercession, Moses prays for mercy rather than judgment, and God relents. Are there situations or people in your life where God may be calling you to intercede and ask for mercy?

4. In Exodus 36, God gave Bezalel and Oholiab wisdom to do all the work that God asked of Moses and the people. God had an assignment, and then provided people and wisdom to have the job done well. Meditate on this. What does this mean to you?

# Week 4
## Reflection & Notes

## Gratitude

# INSPIRATION

I did not grow up in church. My family were CEO Christians (Christmas Easter Only), so I didn't have any foundation in Christ. When I was only eleven, I was already addicted to drugs and pornography. These addictions kicked off a downward spiral leading me to selling drugs and hanging out with gangs.

On Aug 20, 2014, I was locked up and put into jail for breaching a court ordered curfew in place due to a series of convictions for mischief and vandalism. Upon entry I saw a little Gideon's Bible so I grabbed it and began reading the New Testament as well as Psalms and Proverbs.

My girlfriend at the time was in Portugal for the summer so she didn't know I was locked up. However, she called the jail looking for me because her great grandmother, in prayer the night before, told her she saw I was arrested. She also saw that I was reading the Bible and knew I would encounter God and my life would never be the same.

Right then and there, I encountered the love of Jesus so hard I hit the floor, bawling my eyes out. A guy in my cell named Mikey grabbed the phone and told her, "Don't break up with him!" She asked him what was happening. Mickey answered, "I don't know!" just as guards came in, took the phone and told him to get back on the bed. Mikey later told me when they opened the door and ordered him on the bed, he slid to the floor in the presence of God and could not move. It would take some time for me to realize, the moment I hit the floor crying, I was instantly set free and delivered from my addictions, depression, anxiety and suicidal thoughts.

I was ordered to serve two house arrest periods. The first one was three months. I had plenty of time to venture down all the belief systems to find out if what I encountered was actually Jesus or something else. I looked into Islam, Buddhism, atheism, evolution, and more yet I didn't find anything like what I encountered except for other people's encounters with Jesus. This solidified my belief that I had truly encountered Jesus—which meant what the Bible talks about must be true and must be real, including the miracles and signs and wonders.

I joined a group of new believers where we gathered to talk about tough things going on in our lives and in our hearts. Together we went on a journey growing through things we never dealt with. At some point we questioned, why are we not seeing the miracles Smith Wigglesworth saw in his ministry? I was hungry to see the miracles, signs and wonders, so I ordered a bunch of books and teaching resources. I came across *God's Generals* and became convinced that miracles are still occurring today.

The movie *War Room* had just come out and the film emphasized a prayer room so I cleaned up the basement in my house and began to pray there. I prayed there every moment I had telling God I wanted to operate in miracles and healing for His glory.

In my quest I found Dan Mohler's *Love and Forgiveness*, which melted my heart. Then I discovered Todd White's Power and Love Conference and the Love In Action Outreach. I was drawn to seeing regular people experience miracles on the streets, so I flew to Neward, NJ for a conference. On day one I saw people get healed of serious infirmities. I prayed for a man who was completely healed of Parkinson's, free from his 51 pills a day and he was saved and baptized in the Holy Spirit. I prayed for a man's crushed hand and watched bones go back into place. Because of that encounter his son gave his life to Jesus. The power of God is real and for today. I encountered Jesus and my life has never been the same.

~Mark Thompson

# Week 5

"For I am the Lord your God. Consecrate yourselves therefore, and be holy, for I am holy. ~*Leviticus 11:44*

## READING PLAN

| | |
|---|---|
| Day 1: | Exodus 37-40 |
| Day 2: | Leviticus 1-4 |
| Day 3: | Leviticus 5-7 |
| Day 4: | Leviticus 8-11 |
| Day 5: | Leviticus 12-14 |
| Day 6: | Leviticus 15-18 |
| Day 7: | Rest Day/Catch Up |

## *Faith in Action*

Ask yourself if there's anything that may be hindering your relationship with God. Make a list of those things, then take some time and pray a prayer of repentance, asking God to forgive you.

Week 5   Date: _____

# Journal Questions

1. In Leviticus 10, Aaron's two sons brought "strange" fire before God. What does that word "strange" mean in Hebrew? What does this account show or teach us?

2. God asked the people to not sacrifice an unclean beast to Him. What is an unclean beast? (Leviticus 11) Why would He say that to them? What could it represent?

3. Leviticus 17:11 says, "Blood makes atonement for life." Why was the blood being shed so important in the sacrifice? Reflect on how this speaks prophetically of our salvation.

4. Leviticus has a theme of "clean" versus "unclean." Clean in Hebrew means "pure." Unclean means "impure." What could this mean for how we are to live for and worship God?

# Week 5
## Reflection & Notes

## Gratitude

# Inspiration

I had a dream one night that would change my life forever. In the dream, I was dialing 911. When I woke up from the dream, I sprang up because I felt like I had been struck in my chest. I could barely breathe because pain was shooting down my left arm and into my elbow. I was sweating profusely as my heart rate slowed dramatically. I felt disoriented as I stumbled into the living room to pick up the phone and dial 911. My breathing was so shallow I could barely speak. I knew I was dying.

I was drifting in and out of consciousness when the paramedics finally got to me. They put me on a stretcher and that was the last thing I remember before falling into a coma. They contacted my parents, who were four and a half hours away. Everything went from bad to worse. I went into respiratory arrest which caused cardiac arrest. The paramedics worked hard to get me stabilized. While still in the ambulance, I died and they brought me back. They put a tube down my throat to put me on a respirator, which caused me to aspirate and gave me pneumonia in my lung. When they put the IV in, the saline began to leak into the surrounding tissue which created a black, third degree burn. They wrapped it with a bandage.

Dave and Joyce Meyer were my first visitors after waking from the coma. They prayed for me. As they were praying, the doctor issued local anesthesia to deaden an area on my left upper thigh to do a skin graph. They could not put me back to sleep in the condition my body was in. Once my body could handle it, they put me back into a coma. While in the coma, my lung collapsed. This time, they brought my parents in and told them to say their goodbyes.

My parents started a prayer chain through Joyce Meyer Ministries and the distribution department I worked in. As they were praying, they saw three angels enter my hospital room. The third angel stood right in front of where I was laying down. That angel breathed on me with the breath of life. The breath of life filled my lungs and bronchial tubes. From that point on, everything turned around.

I had about thirteen different bags of medicine going through my IV. I was on a ventilator for twelve days. Then they transferred me to the ICU for sixteen days. After that, they placed me in a private room for another week to gain strength to leave the hospital. I was in the hospital a total of twenty-three days. The Lord laid Psalms 23 on my heart to meditate on for the rest of that year.

It has been almost 22 years since then and I am fully recovered from that experience.

By the way, I saw Heaven! While my spirit was out of my body, I saw the paramedics working on me to get me back. Heaven is so beautiful and words cannot really describe what I saw! I saw a garden and it had flower combinations and colors we do not see here on earth. I could walk without destroying the flowers. The peace was otherworldly. Everything was so easy and felt like I was moving without effort. I was also taken into a huge large field of wheat. While there, I saw different scenes from my life: when I was a toddler, a young girl, and throughout my elementary years. These were different moments in my life where I would be outside in my yard, lifting my hands, laughing and singing songs to Jesus, but the difference was now Jesus was there doing this with me. Heaven is real!

*~Stacy McLain*

# Week 6

"The Lord bless you and keep you; the Lord make His face shine upon you and be gracious to you; the Lord lift up His countenance upon you and give you peace. 'So shall they put my name upon the people of Israel, and I will bless them.'" ~*Numbers 6:24-27*

## READING PLAN

| | |
|---|---|
| Day 1: | Leviticus 19-21 |
| Day 2: | Leviticus 22-24 |
| Day 3: | Leviticus 25-27 |
| Day 4: | Numbers 1-3 |
| Day 5: | Numbers 4-6 |
| Day 6: | Numbers 7-8 |
| Day 7: | Rest Day/Catch Up |

## Faith in Action

Make every effort to pronounce the blessing of the Lord over your children or other loved ones this week.

Week 6   Date: _____

# Journal Questions

1. In Leviticus 19, God tells the people to leave some of their crops for the poor. What are ways you could apply this in your life?

2. In Leviticus 25 we read about the Year of Jubilee. Why do you think God put this in place? Is there a principle that applies to us today?

3. In Numbers 6, we learn of the Nazarite vow. What are the three elements of the vow and how might they be significant to our lives today?

4. The priestly blessing (Numbers 6) is a powerful prayer. It's a great prayer to say over people. How could you implement this prayer into your daily or weekly routine?

## Week 6
# Reflection & Notes

# Gratitude

# Inspiration

It started with a mundane tool I couldn't find. In frustration I asked the Lord, "Lord, I know you know where that tool is, can you please tell me?" He responded as clearly as if someone whispered in my ear. I found it exactly where He told me it would be. This conversation became a regular one. I knew it was the Lord's voice because He was always right. Surely there was a bigger purpose for this connection.

After several months God said, "I want you to hear my voice so that when I speak you can hear what I want." He would soon send instructions in a dream followed by a sequence of confirmations. On July 19, 2020, in the midst of Covid, God gave me a dream where I found myself in a Christian facility. An unfamiliar group of people gathered angrily outside to pray against God's people, yet nobody was taking any action to stop them. I led a group outside where we raised our hands to the heavens, lifting the name of Jesus. Crowds joined collectively all over their city. The enemy's work was totally destroyed.

"This is what I want you to do for me. I want you to take the city." I knew God's voice immediately because I had heard Him for the last several months. I felt led to open my Bible to Joshua 8:19. *"Then the men in ambush rose quickly from their place, and when he had stretched out his hand, they ran and captured the city, and they quickly set it on fire."* God wanted me to capture the city for Him. The fire represented the revival He wanted to start.

The last confirmation came when I pulled out a book by Ruth Ward Heflin written in 1990. While praying in Jerusalem she had a vision of "at least 100 stretchers filled with critically ill people. I saw television cameras and reporters and all the major networks there to record the great revival. I saw America ablaze with fire and Dallas, Texas was the center of it."

God wanted believers to stand up against the plans of the enemy. He didn't want us to wait for medicine. He wanted the glory. Satan designed the pandemic for our destruction, but God had a bigger plan. I told my wife, Jules, that we were supposed to pray for our city and the eradication of the virus. We reached out to one person, a retired pastor friend of ours, and told him about the dream. He said he would make a couple of phone calls. Thirty days later, we had over one million people praying around the world on August 19th, 2020. Most of the major networks that carry christian programming around the world carried the event as we prayed live.

What started in my state spread across the country and the world. The evening news interviewed people who stopped what they were doing at 12:00 p.m. that day, which included entire charity organizations, churches, and universities. A rabbi stated he finished a call with leaders across the country and that nations such as Dubai, Egypt, and Israel were participating.

Our small step of obedience exploded into a phenomenon because we responded to the voice of God. The simplest little task can have the largest impact if you allow Him to carry out the details instead of waiting until you come up with a plan. We carried out our best effort and God did what He wanted with it.

It is important to exercise the ability to hear from God and act on it. Your everyday walk with God creates the opportunity to do great things for Him even though it seems you are only involved in mundane things. Our common, everyday obedience always prepares us for greater opportunities.

~Thomas Altemus

# Week 7

"God is not man, that He should lie, or a son of man, that He should change His mind. Has He said, and will He not do it? Or has He spoken, and will He not fulfill it?" ~*Numbers 23:19*

## READING PLAN

| | |
|---|---|
| Day 1: | Numbers 9-12 |
| Day 2: | Numbers 13-15 |
| Day 3: | Numbers 16-19 |
| Day 4: | Numbers 20-22 |
| Day 5: | Numbers 23-26 |
| Day 6: | Numbers 27-29 |
| Day 7: | Rest Day/Catch Up |

## Faith in Action

Repeat this prayer ~ "Dear Lord, help me submit to the process of delay. Help me wait patiently and trust that Your plans for me are perfect and just what I need at this time. Father, I pray for wisdom while on this journey. Help me to not look right or left, but keep my focus on You, the author and finisher of my faith. Amen."

Week 7     Date: _____

# Journal Questions

1. In Numbers 11:1, the people complain incurring God's anger. Another version says "it was evil in the ears of God." What is at the heart of complaining and why does God see it as evil? Are there areas you tend to complain about? What does complaining create in your life?

2. In Numbers 21, we hear of the story of the bronze serpent. This symbol is often used in our medical community even today. Reflect on the elements of the story and how they point to the Cross. What was required for the people to be saved?

3. Many people died in the wilderness because of disobedience to God and His commands. How can this be an example for you and how can you apply it to your life today?

4. In Numbers 23, Balak wanted to curse the Israelites so he called Balaam to come and curse them, but he couldn't do it. Whenever he tried, God would not allow him to curse His chosen people. As a person who believes upon Jesus, you are grafted into His chosen people. Does this encourage you? How can you apply this truth to your walk?

# Week 7
## Reflection & Notes

## Gratitude

# INSPIRATION

God blessed me with three adopted children. My oldest son was severely abused before he was a year old and consequently developed serious mental health and trauma responses. To add to his struggles, he also has high functioning autism.

The strain of raising a child with mental illness is merciless and unrelenting. My wife and I eventually divorced and because it wasn't fair to have the other two children in the same home with Jacoby, I took custody of him and the other two went with their mother.

Jacoby got physically aggressive, acting out in many ways. Being a social worker for fifteen years, I understood what was going on and knew how to navigate the system. I turned to the courts and available resources but we had no support.

God told me to sell everything and move in order to get him help. We moved, but things got drastically worse. I was told to choose between my child or my job. I chose my child. Counseling didn't help and we were trapped in our house 24/7. If we went somewhere he would steal, run away, or physically hurt somebody. He was only thirteen.

Four years prior, I was diagnosed with PTSD by a psychiatrist that told me I needed to get help or I wouldn't survive. In order to be on guard for my son I became hyper-vigilant and began sleeping very little. Things continued to escalate. I installed twenty-one cameras around my house and could not leave it. I resolved to never make a mistake which could cost me, my son, or somebody else. I knew where everything was at all times, especially the knives. I took the guilt upon myself realizing someone could be killed.

One night I found Jacoby in his room with a knife. I took him to the ER where my body finally shut down. Eight hours later I woke up convulsing. Doctors were mystified until they read my records from the Amen Clinic where my psychiatrist predicted that without intervention, my body would go into Trauma Shock. My brain and nervous system stopped communicating. I couldn't talk. I could barely move and shook uncontrollably. I was given three months to survive because I refused to be sent away for treatment. Jacoby was placed in a shelter and I was prescribed bed-rest for eighteen hours each day, only able to stay awake and get up for five minute intervals to stretch. Within three weeks I told God I was ready to go home to Him. Jacoby was safe, my other kids were fine and I felt unable to continue. Then Jesus appeared to me. "I need you to finish what you have been called to be. You are a Gravedigger. You will raise people from the dead like Lazarus. You will raise the physically, mentally and emotionally wounded from the hopelessness and loneliness of their graves. You will speak life into them as a father. If you are going to release this for other people, you need to experience the journey out of the graveyard yourself."

I went on a journey with God. During those three months, I documented everything He taught me. I read Psalms and studied David's cries. My doctor removed the PTSD and Trauma Shock diagnoses from my files. I dove into my calling and poured into other people's lives. Jacoby has now been in treatment for nearly two years and is doing incredibly well. We spend every weekend together. Everyone called my son a monster and urged me to give up, but I loved him with all my heart and was prepared to fight for him until I died. God left the ninety-nine for the one and so He has called me to reach the unreachable and touch the untouchable.

*~Devin Schubert*

# Week 8

"You shall love the Lord your God with all your heart and with all your soul and with all your might." ~*Deuteronomy 6:5*

## READING PLAN

| | |
|---|---|
| Day 1: | Numbers 30-32 |
| Day 2: | Numbers 33-36 |
| Day 3: | Deuteronomy 1-3 |
| Day 4: | Deuteronomy 4-6 |
| Day 5: | Deuteronomy 7-10 |
| Day 6: | Deuteronomy 11-14 |
| Day 7: | Rest Day/Catch Up |

## Faith in Action

Do you believe you're going through a transition, big or small? List steps you can take to be successful in this season. Make a timeline to help you meet your goals.

Week 8     Date: _____

## *Journal Questions*

1. Lot and Esau received their portion before Israel entered into their promised land. Instead, Israel stayed in the wilderness for 40 years before "receiving their portion." Sometimes it looks like others are receiving their blessings first. Does that mean God has forgotten you? Or is He perhaps preparing you for what's to come?

2. In Deuteronomy 6, God gives several practical ways for them to remember His commandments. What are some practical ways that might help you remember what He has said in His Word?

3. What is the point of the "wilderness?" The Isralites wandered for 40 years in the wilderness. What does God say through Moses about this in Deuteronomy 8?

4. How do we recognize a false prophet according to Deuteronomy 13?

# Week 8
## Reflection & Notes

## Gratitude

# Inspiration

It was a miracle crusade night in Uganda, Africa. Thousands gathered to hear the Word of God and to receive their miracles. Others came because they had heard of the miracles that happened the night before. And others were on-lookers, not knowing what to expect. Most certainly there were witches and warlocks present as they usually are on any given crusade night.

This night felt different. There was a sense of expectation in the air. An expectIon of a great move of God. As I preached the word that night, I felt the Lord say to me to release His glory over the people. As I did, the Lord began to download words of knowledge: tumors disappearing, infertility curses nullified, blind eyes open, deaf and dumb set free, foul spirits and demonic oppression broken, in the mighty name of Jesus. Those who were mentally tormented by evil spirits began to manifest.

After releasing the glory of God, I felt led to have those who had received their miracle come to the platform to testify. Suddenly, a mama began to bring her child up the steps of the platform as I was speaking to the crowd. I felt her presence behind me. I immediately turned around and saw her holding her child. I then felt a special anointing surge in me and I heard the Holy Spirit say, "She will walk!" I knew in my spirit I was about to see the Lord perform a miracle.

I looked at the mama and her child and reached out my hand to her and said, "Bring her to me!" The mama immediately brought her to me. While the mom continued to hold her, I directed two of my team members to each put one of their hands on each of the little girl's feet. I declared, "In the mighty name of Jesus, I command the spirit of infirmity and paralysis to come out of her now! Little girl, I command you to walk!" I stretched out my hand and said, "Mama give her to me!" The mom gave me the girl's hands and I immediately assisted her across the platform as she took her very first steps.

Her name was Devine. Devine was a four-year-old girl who had never walked from birth. Devine was miraculously healed that night and walked for the very first time. My eyes were filled with tears and my voice cracked as I testified to the crowd of what had just taken place. Thousands of people witnessed this miracle. Devine's life was transformed from that day forward and she will never be the same. As a result of Devine's miracle, thousands gave their lives to the Lord that night and their lives were transformed forever.

Moving in miracles does not take a superwoman or a superman. It simply takes a person willing to listen to the voice of God and obey without question. It takes obedience and faith to see miracles happen. The Lord's will is always to heal. Sometimes we don't see miracles because we don't believe. Sometimes we don't see miracles because it's not the right time and God is in the process of doing something. Whatever the reason, we should never give up pursuing miracles.

Inevitably your miracle will come. In God's timing it will come. In fact, it's already on the way. He will not leave you and will always back up His Word. When you make a declaration, heaven is mobilized and invades earth. We get to see the kingdom of God come to earth when miracles happen. In heaven there is no sin or infirmity. Let us, together, contend to see a mighty move of God upon the earth today. Let us partner with heaven and co-create with God. Let heaven on earth become our reality.

~Apostle Jessica Z. Maldonado, Founder: Freedom To The Nations - FreedomToTheNations.org

# Week 9

"I call heaven and earth to witness against you today, that I have set before you life and death, blessing and curse. Therefore choose life, that you and your offspring may live," ~*Deuteronomy 30:19*

## READING PLAN

Day 1:    Deuteronomy 15-18
Day 2:    Deuteronomy 19-22
Day 3:    Deuteronomy 23-26
Day 4:    Deuteronomy 27-28
Day 5:    Deuteronomy 29-31
Day 6:    Deuteronomy 32-34
Day 7:    Rest Day/Catch Up

## Faith in Action

Take time to be with the Lord in nature: go for a walk, hike, swim, etc. Focus on being grateful for this beautiful world around you and soak in the presence of your Heavenly Father.

Week 9    Date: _____

## Journal Questions

1. In Deuteronomy 18, God says, "Do not learn to follow the abominations of those nations." What does this mean? What is an abomination? How does this apply to how we worship God today?

2. God tells us not to mix or sow seed together, or wear different fabrics (specifically wool and linen) together? Why? What do you think "pure" worship looks like for us today?

3. In Deuteronomy 27-28, God gives us the blessings and the curses. They are if-then statements. Read through them, reflecting on their relevance for our lives today.

4. Following God's good, set-apart instruction, is not too hard for us (Deuteronomy 30:11). Have you felt at times that His instruction is hard or burdensome? Why do you think this is? How can these verses help us in walking out His commands?

# Week 9
## Reflection & Notes

## Gratitude

# Inspiration

*They shall lift you up in their hands, so that you will not strike your foot against a stone. ~Psalm 91:12*

I was riding my motorcycle along a tiny two lane road called Old Jacksonville Highway. It is the kind of narrow road you drive cautiously to avoid rubbing mirrors with cars in the opposite lane. There are no shoulders on either side of the roadway but a deep bar ditch and one hundred foot pine trees run precariously close to drivers in both directions.

This country road is infamous for head on collisions as there is nowhere to go to escape a crash. Cars pull out of private driveways without warning and are unseen. It is a deadly stretch, even on a clear day.

I planned to meet my wife at her place of business that afternoon. The day was warm and the ride was good. Without warning, the front tire of my Enduro blew out. Rubber pushed itself to one side of the wheel and steel shifted to the other. Uncontrollably, the bike tilted to one side and then the next,. I veered precipitously off the road toward the bar ditch, toward the trees two feet beyond it.

Fighting to get back on the road, I narrowly missed the gaping mouth of the ditch and its trees lined up like hundreds of sinister teeth. I restored my motorcycle back onto solid road only to lean to the left toward oncoming traffic. Fifty feet away I saw it. A 1987, midnight blue Chevy Silverado pickup identical to my granddad's was racing toward me at sixty miles an hour.

There were cars behind me as far as I could see in the mirror. There was an endless string of cars in front of me, coming at me. I couldn't control the bike. I was either going to end up in the ditch on the opposite side of the road or hit the truck head on. I blinked. When I opened my eyes I was on the bar ditch side of the road on my side, in a little driveway. There was not a car in any direction, the bike was still idling and I never touched the ground.

I was in awe, shaken, and perplexed. How did this happen? It was as if someone picked me up, waited for all the cars to pass and set me on the other side of the road peacefully. I know I didn't end up in the ditch or pick up my bike. I somehow made my way back across the other side. I don't remember navigating traffic. There is no explanation how I was in an oncoming lane headed toward a truck yet all the cars passed and I walked away from it. This was intervention outside this realm. There was no passage of time. I closed my eyes and the scene shifted. I had no time to think. It was like a slideshow or a frozen zoom, an abbreviated fraction of time flipped a slide and I was not there. When it was safe, I was back and no one else was around. I imagined the guy driving the truck exclaiming loudly to all his friends later, "I don't know where that motorcycle rider went! He was coming right at me and then he vanished into thin air!"

Later I pushed the bike two miles to a gas station, got the tire back on the wheel and filled it up. Ironically, I never had trouble with that tire again. I can't explain why the tire went flat anymore than I can explain the space time gap. I put it in the hands of an almighty God and His messengers who are able to keep my foot and my bike from hitting stones, and oncoming trucks.

~J Loren Norris

# Week 10

"Have I not commanded you? Be strong and courageous. Do not be frightened, and do not be dismayed, for the Lord your God is with you wherever you go." ~*Joshua 1:9*

## READING PLAN

| | |
|---|---|
| Day 1: | Joshua 1-5 |
| Day 2: | Joshua 6-8 |
| Day 3: | Joshua 9-11 |
| Day 4: | Joshua 12-14 |
| Day 5: | Joshua 15-18 |
| Day 6: | Joshua 19-21 |
| Day 7: | Rest Day/Catch Up |

## Faith in Action

Be kind. Kindness always wins. Do three random acts of kindness this week.

Week 10   Date: _____

## Journal Questions

1. Four times Joshua is told to be strong and courageous (three by God, once by the people.) Are there areas in your life where you need to be reminded of this same thing?

2. Before Joshua fights the battle of Jericho, he has an encounter with the Lord (Joshua 5:31-15.) Reread this encounter. What can you learn from this and apply to your life today?

3. Why did God tell Joshua and the Israelites to put everyone from the nations "under the ban?" What do you think this represents?

4. Sometimes there are things we are asked to do by God, and we know He wants us to do it, but it may not make sense to our human understanding. Are you willing to walk in obedience even if it doesn't make sense? Why or why not? If you hesitate, why? What can you do or choose to implement to fully walk in obedience?

# Week 10
## Reflection & Notes

## Gratitude

# INSPIRATION

I was only ten when an aneurysm ruptured in my brain and caused a hemorrhagic stroke. I went into a coma that lasted for eight weeks. When I woke up I was deaf, paralyzed and did not even know who my parents were. Starting from scratch, I required physical therapy to relearn how to read, write and even speak again. Because I was now deaf, I had to learn sign language.

As that first year of therapy came to a close, doctors prepared to release me into a rehab facility. However, just before that transfer was completed my brain bled again. While they hastily prepared me for surgery I flatlined and died.

After nearly thirty minutes of resuscitation attempts my mother was called in to pay her last respects and see me one last time. Sometime within that thirty minute period I remember a very bright light extinguishing my vision of anything else around it. It was like peering directly into the sun. A hand thrust itself toward me—into me. It was hot white, brighter than the sun, and it grabbed me with such force I gasped choking down my first breath of air. Thirty minutes after I was pronounced dead my mother heard my sharp inhale. I heard her weeping and I knew that the white hand had rescued me from death. I was not a christian, nor did I grow up in a christian home, so I did not know the Lord yet, nor recognize the hand of God clenched tightly around me.

That was not the first time the Lord's hand was upon me. While my mother was raising my older sister she decided one child was enough. When she became pregnant with my brother she decided to abort him. At the abortion clinic they told her she was having twins, however she insisted a prior ultrasound revealed only one male fetus and they proceeded with the abortion. Doctors said I was literally tucked away high in the uterus as if being nurtured and protected by it. The abortionist tools never reached my body when they took my brother. Her obstetrician said he couldn't explain it and called it a miracle. My mother recognized the marvel for what it was and did not pursue another abortion.

Ten years later I was lifted from the grave and eventually walked out of rehab on my own. After countless healing miracles my ears were eventually opened and I was no longer deaf. The consequences of my illness were nothing in the hands of a powerful God, yet I still did not know Him.

The Lord would pull me out of another pit before I would recognize His hand at work in my life. A few years later, my alcohol and drug addicted father told me it was time for me to get a job to pay off the crippling medical bills...and because he needed money for drugs.

At age thirteen I was trafficked through our neighbor's trucking company. I was consequently branded, made a member of the cult, and subjected to satanic ritual abuse. I saw no salvation outside of death and jumped off a bridge to take my own life. This time God used the hands of a young believer to draw me out of the depths of that river and show me His Word. When I accepted Christ I saw that same brilliant illuminated hand again and I recognized it as the Lord's hand that had come to save me from death. God tells us in Isaiah 41:10, *"Fear not, for I am with you; be not dismayed, for I am your God; I will strengthen you, I will help you, I will uphold you with my righteous right hand."* I know His hand preserved me for such a time as this.

~Christine Barterbonia

# Week 11

"And if it is evil in your eyes to serve the Lord, choose this day whom you will serve, whether the gods your fathers served in the region beyond the river, or the gods of the Amorites in whose land you dwell. But as for me and my house, we will serve the Lord."
~*Joshua* 24:15

## READING PLAN

| | |
|---|---|
| Day 1: | Joshua 22-24 |
| Day 2: | Judges 1-4 |
| Day 3: | Judges 5-7 |
| Day 4: | Judges 8-10 |
| Day 5: | Judges 11-13 |
| Day 6: | Judges 14-17 |
| Day 7: | Rest Day/Catch Up |

## Faith in Action

Take some time this week to remember how God has blessed you. Write a list of those blessings.

Week 11  Date: _____

# Journal Questions

1. God was trying the Israelites to see if they would follow His ways. (Judges 2) God will test us to see if we will stand up for Him and His Ways. Sometimes we are quick to blame the Enemy for everything. What if sometimes it is God testing us? Have you been tested at a particular moment in your walk?

2. In Judges 16, Delilah asks Samson three times for the source of his strength. After the first two, she unsuccessfully attempts to have him captured. Even after this, he reveals the source of his strength to her. Why do you think this is and what can we learn from it? (Consider especially verse 16:20.)

3. Gideon set up a shoulder garment to gaze upon, and it became a snare. Our flesh so desperately desires to worship a "thing." What things have you elevated in your life that need to come down today?

4. Even just a few generations after the Exodus, the Israelites quickly forgot all that God had done to bless them. What about in our generation, and our own life? Why do you think it is so easy to forget all that He has done?

# Week 11
## Reflection & Notes

## Gratitude

## Inspiration

There was a man in our church group that had significant health problems, so I started studying scripture on healing. Six months later, while waiting in our backyard for our small group to arrive, my six year old son Andrae climbed a basketball hoop and hung on the rim as it fell over, crushing his hand.

The physicians at urgent care said a metacarpal bone in his hand broke in half. I then heard the Lord say to me, "I wanted you to study healing for you. I want Andrae to be a Pastor, so I need him to see my power and my glory."

I shared this word with my son who trusted the Lord. I fasted for the next three days and my son chose to fast for one day. He then insisted he was healed. That night at our small group he took off his splint and played basketball. The next day at his casting appointment the orthopedist looked at his newest x-ray and remarked that he could not explain why there was no sign of a break.

My son testified that God healed him. He got to see the glory of God and stand in faith but God was preparing me for something bigger. Soon after, I got pregnant with our seventh child. The Holy Spirit told me I was going to experience something very hard but to trust Him.

At eleven weeks I started bleeding profusely. I sat in a pool of blood on the way to the ER calling my doctor who told me to go home, I was miscarrying and there was nothing they could do. The trail of blood led all the way to the bathtub where I soaked in every one of the healing scriptures claiming my own healing, believing His word.

The bleeding stopped but every week they told me the subchorionic hemorrhage they'd found meant that that embryonic sack was detaching from my uterus and a miscarriage was imminent. Every week I had to get into my scripture and claim "the Lord will not take this baby. I believe you, I know you'll heal me," but I did not see the healing.

We were at the movies when I went into labor. After giving birth to a baby girl, I was hospitalized for five weeks and during that time God gave me the number forty. I thought that meant forty weeks, but I gave birth at twenty nine weeks. Packing to go home without my baby laying in the NICU was heartbreaking but God reassured me, "Not 40 weeks, 40 days." I knew then my baby was coming home soon.

Doctors insisted our daughter would require 120 days in the hospital, but the Lord told me 40 and I clung to that promise. On the 38th day doctors told me she wasn't doing as well as they had hoped and it would be several more weeks. The next day as we walked toward her bed, the doctors came to us and said, "Your daughter's going home tomorrow!"

The Lord prepared me through my son's broken hand to know that God will do what He says He will do. He used that accident to bring glory to His name for my son's faith, but He also exercised the measure of my own faith to prepare me for what was to come and to impart absolute confidence that He will bring about every one of His promises, including those things we assume are too much for Him.

~Karissa Collins

# Week 12

"Then she fell on her face, bowing to the ground, and said to him, "Why have I found favor in your eyes, that you should take notice of me, since I am a foreigner?" ~Ruth 2:10

## READING PLAN

| | |
|---|---|
| Day 1: | Judges 18-21 |
| Day 2: | Ruth 1-4 |
| Day 3: | 1 Samuel 1-3 |
| Day 4: | 1 Samuel 4-7 |
| Day 5: | 1 Samuel 8-11 |
| Day 6: | 1 Samuel 12-14 |
| Day 7: | Rest Day/Catch Up |

## Faith in Action

Take some time this week to look at what is contributing to any stress in your life. What action steps will you take to move forward with less stress?

Week 12      Date: _____

## Journal Questions

1. Judges is a downward spiral culminating in the last verse of the book, "Everyone did what was right in his own eyes." How do we keep ourselves from the same pattern?

2. Ruth was a foreigner, and then married Boaz, which grafted her into his family. Jesus was in the lineage of Boaz. Why is this important and what insights can we gather from it as believers today?

3. When Samuel was young, he didn't recognize God was speaking to him until the third time. Do you know how to recognize God's voice? What can you do to hear Him more?

4. King Saul messed up numerous times. What was the common theme of his transgressions?

# Week 12
## Reflection & Notes

## Gratitude

# INSPIRATION

I ministered to Angel for many years. She was heavily addicted to narcotics and heroin, but she was a beautiful girl and I knew that the seeds I planted were not sown in barren soil. Her mother gave her narcotics when she was a young child. She suffered from a hip displacement and required several surgeries as well as a steel rod between her legs. As she got older she graduated to injecting narcotics into her veins. She shot up heroin and used anything she could get her hands on. She often called me at 2:00 or 3:00 in the morning, broken and crying.

One night she called me crying hysterically on the phone. She was pregnant. Despite her lifestyle, she had moral convictions about abortion and chose to keep her baby. She understood she needed to stay clean, but her soul was in a tug of war and she could not quit using. I knew if she could stop using drugs by a certain point in her pregnancy, the baby would develop unharmed so I devised a plan.

I drove to Missouri where Angel was excited to see me and casually invited her to join me to go to the store and get something to eat. She climbed into my passenger seat and I drove past stores and strip malls, continuing on to a conference in Kansas City. The Onething Conference took place over the course of several days, culminating on New Years where thousands gathered in the stadium to praise Jesus. I had already registered our names and reserved a hotel room. During our stay, she wouldn't have access to drugs so she couldn't use them. I was believing in a miracle!

Once the truth behind my plan was discovered she insisted she could not endure a conference in her pregnant state and demanded I take her home. I could see she was physically uncomfortable and I knew she could not sit and listen to speakers, but there was a ministry room where Misty Edwards was leading worship, so I instructed her to lay on the floor with a pillow and blanket.

By this time all the drugs were out of her body. She was in a lot of pain, specifically her hip. Detoxing hurts all the way to the marrow as the body starts purging and she laid on the floor in misery. Misty saw her and pressed in, singing about the Lord being a deliverer and healer, singing about the darkness fleeing. I watched the room fill with God's glory rolling, billowing amber gold clouds moving towards heaven.

A side door opened suddenly, bright light illuminating the open space where a very tall, beautiful woman, with a crown of glory, emerged and glided across the room towards Angel and me. Angel lay in a nearly fetal position, her hip facing upward as the angelic woman spoke a German sounding prayer language over her. I stepped aside to allow what God had brought. The prayer language song flowed and floated over Angel as the ethereal woman bent down and put her hand on the hip... then disappeared.

Angel cried out to the Lord thanking Him with tears that poured out like oil. She sat up exclaiming, "I'm not in pain. How did she know?" "That was not a woman that was an angel. The Lord sent her!" I exclaimed.

She was able to attend the rest of the conference praising the Lord and ringing in the New Year and went home completely detoxed. Her ten pound baby boy was born healthy and she allowed me the honor of naming him Titus.

~Amber Pearl Anderson

# Week 13

"Then David said to the Philistine, "You come to me with a sword and with a spear and with a javelin, but I come to you in the name of the Lord of hosts, the God of the armies of Israel, whom you have defied." ~1 Samuel 17:45

## READING PLAN

| | |
|---|---|
| Day 1: | 1 Samuel 15-17 |
| Day 2: | 1 Samuel 18-21 |
| Day 3: | 1 Samuel 22-25 |
| Day 4: | 1 Samuel 26-28 |
| Day 5: | 1 Samuel 29-31 |
| Day 6: | 2 Samuel 1-3 |
| Day 7: | Rest Day/Catch Up |

## Faith in Action

Pray and ask God to help you trust Him in all you do.

Week 13                    Date: _____

# *Journal Questions*

1. We often hear the verse "to obey is better than sacrifice" quoted. Do you have any examples from your own life of where this verse might apply?

2. Saul used witchcraft to call up Samuel the prophet from the dead because he felt distant from God and wanted a "quick fix" answer. This is deliberately against God's Word. Have you ever desired a "quick fix" answer so badly that you've deliberately disobeyed to get an answer? How did it turn out?

3. King David had the men divide the spoils between those who fought and those who stayed to protect their stuff. Some men were upset that it wasn't fair. What do you think? Have you ever compared your situation to others and felt like it was not fair? How can this story help with those feelings?

4. What can we learn from how David treats Saul in 1 Samuel 24? Are there any "Sauls" in your life that you can apply these lessons to?

# Week 13
## Reflection & Notes

## Gratitude

# Inspiration

My wife and I have a home on Lake Winnisquam in New Hampshire. We have a small fish and ski boat and decided to take our two youngest girls, ages nine and twelve, out on the water for the day. We were low on fuel so I proceeded immediately to the nearest gas station on the marina, maneuvering the boat cautiously through the "No Wake Zone" that lay between the station and where we were docked. I pulled up to the pier where an attendant was waiting to pump my gas. I looked out toward the lake to discover the entire horizon had grown pitch black. Dark, ominous clouds seemed to replicate themselves, rolling toward us like an army in pursuit.

Marine Patrol seemed to materialize out of thin air as they sped toward us with lights flashing. The attendant pulled the nozzle from my tank suddenly and said, "You have to get out of here." A Brooklyn native, I was new to boating and confused. What I did not understand then is that dangerous storms form quickly on large lakes literally out of nowhere and follow the body of water. With lives at stake, the patrol yelled into their speakers at the countless boats scattered on the water to disregard the no wake zone and leave the area as quickly as possible. "Everybody get out of here at full speed NOW! GO!!"

The day had been beautiful, but without warning the weather progressed quickly to a little wind and then a few clouds which quickly morphed to blacken the sky. Hurricane winds announced their fury. We felt the wrath of the wind as it pushed our boat against the gas dock. I could not simply gun it because ahead of me was land. I needed to back up to turn and only then could we make our escape. However, the force of the wind pushed our boat sideways at full speed toward the opposite dock only fifty feet away. My wife and I watched in horror as the dock accelerated toward us. My girls were crying, lighting bolts were striking and we were seconds away from smashing into a pier. Then, inexplicably, an extremely large man appeared out of thin air exactly where we were about to hit the dock. In one fluid motion, he swooped his arms toward us and pushed the boat away from him, allowing me to turn and take off. My wife and I looked back to get another glimpse at the man who just saved our lives but he disappeared as quickly as he arrived on the scene. There was a long J-shaped dock that he would have had to navigate but he was gone like a flash of lightning. It didn't make sense.

The lake was full of boats fleeing the area as quickly as our engines could take us. The image around me was surreal and felt like a war scene. I drove my boat toward the dock by my house as quickly as possible. By the grace of God, my neighbor's daughter was standing there waiting for us, rope in hand, lassoing it and securing our boat to the dock. This was another Godsend! I struggled to tie up as lightning was striking in every direction. We were able to run inside to safety because of her assistance.

I think about that man on the dock that day and it doesn't make any physical sense. A man cannot simply push a 21' boat even when the water is still, let alone when it's coming at high speed with hurricane force winds. He didn't just stop my boat from hitting the dock, he pushed it back with force. That was no ordinary man that vanished as soon as he saved our lives. I can't explain what happened. There is no physical, human explanation for it except the hand of God.

~Peter Nieves

# Week 14

*"Be of good courage, and let us be courageous for our people, and for the cities of our God, and may the Lord do what seems good to him." ~2 Samuel 10:12*

## READING PLAN

| | |
|---|---|
| Day 1: | 2 Samuel 4-8 |
| Day 2: | 2 Samuel 9-12 |
| Day 3: | 2 Samuel 13-15 |
| Day 4: | 2 Samuel 16-18 |
| Day 5: | 2 Samuel 19-21 |
| Day 6: | 2 Samuel 22-24 |
| Day 7: | Rest Day/Catch Up |

## Faith in Action

Recount blessings that God has already given you and done in your life. Give Him praise for what He has already done for you, even if you are walking through a season of challenges.

Week 14       Date: _____

## *Journal Questions*

1. King David was faithful to God and His ways. He went through hard times, but David never swayed from his faithfulness to God. When times get challenging what do you tend to do?

2. "Why have you despised the Word of God to do evil in His eyes?" (2 Samuel 12:9) When we choose evil, or go against God's Word, to Him, we are despising His Word. Have you been guilty of this? Confess, repent and know He forgives quickly. How can we protect ourselves from despising His Word?

3. King David was the "apple of God's eye." He was hand-picked by God and would carry the lineage of Jesus. Yet, he sinned and fell short more than once. What do you notice about King David when he fell short and sinned against God? What example does that give us?

4. The final chapter of 2 Samuel records that David was determined to number the people in Israel. Scripture tells us that the Lord was displeased with him for doing this. Are you determined to count something that the Lord may be displeased with?

# Week 14
## Reflection & Notes

## Gratitude

# Inspiration

Five years ago, I caught the flu and went to urgent care where they prescribed antibiotics. Within a couple of hours of my first dose, I lost feeling in both of my legs and couldn't walk. I was rushed to the hospital where doctors discovered one of the antibiotics had caused my body to be filled with blood clots.

Doctors hurried me into emergency surgery; however, during the operation, my left leg developed "compartment syndrome." My leg was so swollen it was about to burst due to the pressure restricting blood flow and preventing oxygen from reaching the nerves and muscles. The surgeon cut my infected leg open on both sides to relieve the pressure and try to save it. Afterward he told me he had never witnessed anything like it in all his years of surgery and I was lucky to be alive.

That was my first miracle.

He then informed me that while he had removed all the blood clots, the surgery had been unsuccessful in saving my leg and they were preparing for amputation. Because of the trauma my body had gone through, the physicians chose to wait a few days before the next procedure. For the next two days I prayed, visualized, and pictured God miraculously healing me and returning my leg and body to normal. I let the doctors and nurses do their thing, but I remained focused on my healing miracle.

On day three my leg and foot came back to life. I still couldn't feel it, but the surgeon was able to find a very faint pulse. There had been no circulation for two days and it was black, blue, green and purple, but that morning the color completely returned, and they found one faint pulse. By the afternoon they found two pulses. The surgeon told me, "Somehow, we can't explain it, your leg and foot are alive. You get to keep your leg." By this point my room was full of doctors, surgeons, and nurses trying to figure out "how" this had happened!

I pointed to heaven; it was my second miracle.

Then the surgeon, who had absolutely no bedside manner, said to me, "Well, you get to keep your leg, but you might have been better off with a prosthetic. You still don't have feeling and based on all the nerve damage, we don't know when or if you will ever regain feeling, so you're probably going to be a gimp for the rest of your life."

That was the first time in three days I cried, but I decided God already gave me two miracles, so I was not going to give up.

The same surgeon told me the two huge wounds would not heal themselves, I would require plastic surgery and skin grafts for them to heal. I could see the muscles and ligaments inside my leg, but I didn't get discouraged and continued to pray over my body everyday while learning how to care for my own wounds.

I diligently followed the physical therapist's instructions and at 2 ½ months I regained some feeling in my ankle. Even without feeling the in my leg and foot, I learned how to walk again in only six weeks. New skin grew over both wounds which they said was not possible, and they healed on their own without surgery in seven months. I was told if I did not get full feeling back within 12 months I would never get it back, however, after 18 months I regained full feeling to my leg.

I learned how to walk and dance. I am not a gimp. God pulls from the pit, not the pulpit. He pulled me from the pit for a reason. It's up to me to honor my three miracles and cultivate that purpose.

~Ann Nickell

# Week 15

"Let your heart therefore be wholly true to the Lord our God, walking in his statutes and keeping his commandments, as at this day."
~1 Kings 8:61

## READING PLAN

| | |
|---:|:---|
| Day 1: | 1 Kings 1-2 |
| Day 2: | 1 Kings 3-6 |
| Day 3: | 1 Kings 7-8 |
| Day 4: | 1 Kings 9-11 |
| Day 5: | 1 Kings 12-14 |
| Day 6: | 1 Kings 15-17 |
| Day 7: | Rest Day/Catch Up |

## Faith in Action

Pray. Pray for God to move through you to spread His gift of grace and mercy to others this week.

Week 15      Date: _____

## Journal Questions

1. King Solomon was one of the wisest people to walk the earth and yet he still fell into the lust of the flesh and massive sin. He had hundreds of wives that turned his heart away from the one true God and His ways. How can we succeed where this wise man failed?

2. When building the temple, no hammer or chisel was heard in the temple of God (1 Kings 6:7). They had great reverence toward the set-apart place where He would meet the people. What great reverence and fear of Him they had! What are some ways that you can revere God in a similar way?

3. Read and meditate on King Solomon's prayer in 1 Kings 8. What do you see?

4. What can we learn from the faith and trust that the widow had during her encounter with Elijah the prophet in 1 Kings 17?

# Week 15
## Reflection & Notes

## Gratitude

# Inspiration

I muttered, "One more day," as I braced for the last leg of my journey on the greyhound bus. Home was Texas, my parents and everything I knew. New York was a wild city that scared me with loud cars, stale cigarettes, and people I didn't know. My husband was there but I was twenty years old, four months pregnant, and nothing seemed right with no way to fix it.

The world was going crazy. I thought God had bigger issues on His hands than my little frustrations so I didn't bother Him. I had put God into such a tiny box that He couldn't move and I had zero faith in His ability to multitask. When attending church events I would anticipate a word from heaven, yet everyone else seemed to receive prophetic words as I shrank a little lower on the sidelines waiting in vain. I felt small. I felt uniquely forgotten, unseen and unheard.

Feeling no recognition from God, I lost my connection to Him. I was lukewarm, attending church services only out of respect for my parents and a perceived obligation. My grandmother was a preacher and my mother an evangelist, but I believed I missed the mark and I couldn't pray hard enough to correct my course. Truth be told, I married my husband out of defiance to a church community that didn't approve of him in his backslidden state. I worried now that he was not ready to be a father.

I eyed the greyhound as a line was beginning to form in front of it. One more day. Stretching my back, I summoned the courage to advance towards it. I felt very pregnant and uncomfortable, sitting for protracted periods, but the harassment I endured on that bus the last two days, most notably by a man high on drugs, was what had me pregnancy mad. Everything and everyone on that bus had severed my last nerve.

In my agitated state, I noticed the lady in front of me waiting to board. This lady had a radiating light emanating from within her, shining so brightly around her, she appeared to glow. She wasn't the traditional Hollywood beauty, yet she radiated something supernatural. In tan shorts, a maroon t-shirt complete with vest and a backpack, in the manner of Laura Croft she appeared ready to trudge through the jungles. Her short brown hair tied back in a bandana revealed an average, 35-year-old face. In earthly terms she was so ordinary she was almost plain, yet she was gorgeous. My eyes saw her common features, yet my heart and mind overrode what I was seeing and recorded something else. Transfixed by her light, I commented on her beauty. She smiled and replied, "That is just the supernatural presence of the Lord. What you are seeing is the Glory of God. He loves us all so very much that He cares about even the smallest detail of your life."

Peace. Love. Joy. I inhaled and they washed over my body. All the issues with my husband and pregnancy and life drained away. The stress was gone and I could breathe. I couldn't even remember why I was so irritated with my fellow passengers.

As I boarded the bus, I decided I needed more time in that radiant woman's presence, and hoped to find an empty seat beside her. I walked past row after row but the beautiful passenger was nowhere to be found. Nevertheless, as I settled into an empty row, I sat down as if on my Heavenly Father's lap knowing I meant everything to Him. My issues became insignificant because in my importance to God, nothing else mattered. Heaven had reached me on that greyhound bus that day.

~Crystal Jordan

# Week 16

"He said, "Do not be afraid, for those who are with us are more than those who are with them." ~*2 Kings 6:16*

## READING PLAN

| | |
|---|---|
| Day 1: | 1 Kings 18-20 |
| Day 2: | 1 Kings 21-22 |
| Day 3: | 2 Kings 1-3 |
| Day 4: | 2 Kings 4-6 |
| Day 5: | 2 Kings 7-9 |
| Day 6: | 2 Kings 10-12 |
| Day 7: | Rest Day/Catch Up |

## Faith in Action

Smile. You never know who you are influencing.

## Journal Questions

1. In 2 Kings 1, only the third captain's life is spared. What can we learn from his approach? How do we apply it to our lives today?

2. 2 Kings 5 tells us the story of Naaman, commander of the army for Aram, a nation not of Israel. What can we learn about God's heart in this story? Was Naaman an Israelite or a non-believer? Why did he first question what he was told to do to be healed?

3. Elisha prayed and asked God to open his servant's eyes to see the horses and chariots of fire around the army that had encircled them. How does this encourage you? Is there a time when you knew you had protection surrounding you that wasn't visible to the human eye?

4. What was the difference between the kings that did evil in the eyes of God and those that did good? What was evil in the eyes of God?

# Week 16
## Reflection & Notes

## Gratitude

# Inspiration

Shortly after our second daughter Liesel was born we knew something was wrong. When she was just three weeks old her right eye protruded out of its socket. It was springtime, so her pediatrician wrote it off as allergies, "You just notice it more because she's so tiny." She promptly prescribed Benadryl and sent us away.

A week later, every time Liesel cried or fussed her eye protruded exponentially more. Within weeks we thought if she sneezed her eye would come out of its socket. My wife insisted it was not allergies, so we were referred to an ophthalmologist who told us her eye was fine but something lay behind it and referred us to a pediatric oncologist.

Dr. Dom gave us devastating news, "Based on my thirty years of experience, we are dealing with a cancerous tumor." After many tests she determined Liesel had ocular melanoma, but insisted they could not do the necessary biopsy and extensive MRI until she was at least six months old so they could administer anesthesia.

We waited helplessly for three months which seemed like three years, but the day came at last when the MRI confirmed what they suspected. Dr. Dom stated unequivocally, "The best case scenario would be to remove her eye and optic nerve because the cancer is not in the surrounding tissue." This was hard news to absorb. Liesel would face a life without her right eye with all of the practical and cosmetic implications, so we prayed before deciding to proceed. We were dependent on prayer throughout Liesel's illness and people came from all over the country to pray and lay hands on her.

Surgery was scheduled but a new scan revealed the tumor was stable and not growing so they decided it was best to wait until she was a year old. At last they scheduled her operation. I asked for one last scan two days prior so that the surgeon could study her tumor beforehand.

We had had several of these scans by this point and they typically took forty-five minutes. They carted her away and we waited. Forty-five minutes came and went. One hour. One and a half hours. Our nerves counted the seconds now. Two hours. The suspenseful wait was now three times longer than normal. At two hours and five minutes the oncologist, her partner, the surgeon, and the imaging tech came into the waiting room. Dr. Dom had obviously been crying, her face swollen as she carried three scans. We expected the worst and my wife was hysterical. They helped us regain our composure and laid out the brain scans on a coffee table. Two copies of the current one and one from five weeks ago.

Dr. Dom told us, "The tumor is no longer a tumor. It is no longer there. I cannot explain it, and in my thirty years of practicing medicine I have never seen anything like it. There may be something to your God." What remained was a mere cluster of cells called a hemangioma also known as a "strawberry" that had rapidly diminished over a few weeks' time. Liesel's white blood count that had been significantly elevated for months was now within normal range. This was a medically verified miracle!

We learned to lament in the greatest season of our lives. We lost everything that year in an avalanche of financial ruin as my wife and I both heard God audibly proclaim, "You are going to choose Who you are going to serve."

My God is a God of restoration. We went from being bankrupt and homeless to fantastic jobs and a 5000 square foot brick home. God restored everything and more. The more is a peaceful, loving, compassionate home with transformed lives that can better help grow the kingdom because we now have a testimony.

-Benjamin L. Foust

# Week 17

"But you shall fear the Lord your God, and he will deliver you out of the hand of all your enemies." ~2 Kings 17:39

## READING PLAN

| | |
|---|---|
| Day 1: | 2 Kings 13-15 |
| Day 2: | 2 Kings 16-18 |
| Day 3: | 2 Kings 19-22 |
| Day 4: | 2 Kings 23-25 |
| Day 5: | 1 Chronicles 1-3 |
| Day 6: | 1 Chronicles 4-6 |
| Day 7: | Rest Day/Catch Up |

## Faith in Action

Make up your mind to show kindness to those who have not been so kind to you.

Week 17    Date: _____

## *Journal Questions*

1. King Saul is remembered for consulting a medium. What pushed Saul to do this and why are we to stay away from them? What "mediums" do people seek in our day?

2. Many times new kings would come in and attempt to change things back to God's ways. However, they rarely took down the "high places" *(2 Kings 14:4.)* What is a high place? How is this relevant in our modern day?

3. What high places are you keeping "up" in your life that you know He's asking you to take down?

4. Judah and Israel became two separate nations and both were exiled because of their disobedience. Where were they exiled and for how long? Did they ever come out of exile? *(2 Kings 17 & 24)*

# Week 17
# Reflection & Notes

# Gratitude

# INSPIRATION

Let me tell you about the time God said, "LIVE," and I did!

In the Fall of 2010, I was driving home and was only two streets away from pulling in the driveway. I had kicked off my shoes, calling it a night, and then suddenly found myself on the way to Shock Trauma where doctors were fighting to save my life. It had been a horrific car accident. So horrific, my car flipped several times before landing right side up. I can remember climbing out of the passenger side window before collapsing on the side of the road in severe pain. I was in too much pain to move.

By the grace of God, one of our neighbors went for a drive around the neighborhood at 10pm. He found me on the side of the road, unconscious. Minutes later, I was at the local ER. They didn't feel equipped to save me so they sent me to Shock Trauma because I had so much internal bleeding. I didn't realize until then all ER's are not the same. There are ER's and there are Trauma Centers for more life-threatening cases requiring a team of physicians. The latter was my case.

I recall asking the doctors at Shock Trauma, "Am I going to make it?" They responded, "We don't know." I had many injuries; hematoma, pneumothorax, six broken ribs, a spliced spleen, and a severely damaged liver. The liver was my main problem. The doctors told my husband, "It was as if someone took her liver and lifted it up and then threw it on the ground. There are so many splices in it." They would need to do an extensive laser surgery to put my liver back together. Doctors also said I would need to be completely still the entire time. As they wheeled me into the surgery room, the song, "What a Beautiful Word" played in the background. To this day, this song takes me back, reminding me of the hope I gripped onto that day and never let go of.

After the liver surgery, an infection took hold of my liver. Doctors told my husband I was not going to make it unless they put a drain in my liver. They said it was a risky procedure with no guarantee it would work. I would have to remain there for several more months. At this point, I had already been there two and a half weeks, remembering very little of that time as I was on so many pain meds. My family was devastated, scared, and desperate for me to be okay.

The day prior to my liver drain surgery, my husband called his workplace to share updates with his colleague. She said to him, "Pray Ezekiel 16:6 over her!" The passage reads, "And when I passed by you and saw you struggling in your own blood, I said to you in your blood, 'Live!'" She told him it worked for her nephew. My husband, already at the hospital with a roomful of visitors, including our pastor and children, formed a circle around me. Our pastor read Ezekiel 16:6 over me and everyone prayed. I vaguely remember thinking during their prayer circle, "I wish I could take their fear and pain away."

As I was being prepped for surgery the next morning, the trauma doctors arrived saying, "It's inexplicable! Nothing short of a miracle! The infection is gone! She will make it." It has been almost twelve years since my accident. God said, "Live" and I've been living ever since. And I will continue to live the abundant life until He calls me home!

~Michelle Rene' Hammer, MS, LCPC

# Week 18

"Seek the Lord and his strength; seek his presence continually!"
~1 Chronicles 16:11

## READING PLAN

| | |
|---|---|
| Day 1: | 1 Chronicles 7-9 |
| Day 2: | 1 Chronicles 10-13 |
| Day 3: | 1 Chronicles 14-17 |
| Day 4: | 1 Chronicles 18-21 |
| Day 5: | 1 Chronicles 22-24 |
| Day 6: | 1 Chronicles 25-26 |
| Day 7: | Rest Day/Catch Up |

## Faith in Action

Take a moment to confess your sins to the Lord and humble yourself before Him.

Week 18  Date: _____

# Journal Questions

1. Why do you think it bothered David's wife, Michal, when he danced before the Lord? *(1 Chronicles 15:29)* In what ways was she similar to her father Saul?

2. King David had a powerful prayer in 1 Chronicles 16. Read through the prayer again and write down what aspects of the prayer bring specific encouragement to you today.

3. As leaders, the kings set the tone for how their people would follow the Lord. What tone are you setting in areas where you have influence?

4. Kings often chose not to rely on God, but instead looked to other things. How often have you made this same mistake? In what ways can you improve in this area?

# Week 18
## Reflection & Notes

## Gratitude

# Inspiration

Growing up in an Amish family and community gave me a great start in life. I had parents who loved me, provided for me, taught me to love God, love others and work hard. The foundation for my life was rock solid. My theology was "Life is good, God is harsh." If I was good, He would bless me. If I was bad, He would be angry with me.

My whole world came crashing down the day our sweet 19-month-old, Angela Joy, was killed instantly by my sister who was driving a tractor loading and unloading sand for my dad. We were traumatized and in shock. Angie.....gone.....in a split second. It was more than I could bear. I sank into emotional pain and spiritual confusion which was a world I never knew existed. I asked the age-old question..."Why, God?" My husband and I drifted apart and silently existed. I did not have the vocabulary to express my grief and was embarrassed if anyone saw me crying. I spent many nights on the couch crying myself to sleep exhausted from the grief I was holding inside. I believed if I prayed long enough that my grief would disappear. "Weeping may endure for the night, but joy comes in the morning." But joy in the morning never came.

I asked God to please bring someone into my life I could talk to. I believed God had answered my prayer when my pastor saw my sadness and asked me to come to his office. I went to see him, poured out my heart and felt comforted in his presence. When leaving his office, he took advantage of me and preyed on my broken and grieving soul. Not knowing he was a sexual predator and knowing nothing about sexual abuse, I left his office confused by what he said and did. How could I feel comforted by him and in an instant feel confused and silenced? I knew I could never tell anyone because nobody would believe me, so I decided to keep it a secret. The price I paid for that one secret led to six years of sexual abuse, more than 20 years of depression, being an emotionally absent mom, an unfaithful wife and having a dysfunctional family. I hated who I had become. I believed I was unlovable, unforgivable, and unchangeable. I wept my way through seven years of darkness and shame. I was afraid of my perpetrator. I was afraid if I told my husband he would divorce me. I was afraid God had given up on me.

One day while I was praying, God told me it was time to get up off my knees and face my fears and tell my husband Jonas about my secret life. This went against every fiber of my being. Praise God my faith was more powerful than my fear. That moment, even though every emotion and thought was telling me I can't do this. Fear will keep you in its clutches as long as you let it. Fear paralyzes, faith liberates! If I would not have obeyed God that day and pushed through my fear I would never have experienced the supernatural life or fulfilled the purpose God had planned for me. The confession I made to my husband was a small, but powerful miracle. It began the work of redemption in my heart and his. Over time, our family was restored. God created "Auntie Anne's Pretzels," which grew around the world changing the lives of thousands of people with its own miracle story. What I know today is: Life is hard, God is good. And I am not confused anymore. Confession can create miracles in your life, you just have to trust God and do it.

*-Anne Beiler, Founder of Auntie Anne's Pretzels, Author and Speaker*

# Week 19

*"You will not need to fight in this battle. Stand firm, hold your position, and see the salvation of the Lord on your behalf, O Judah and Jerusalem." ~2 Chronicles 20:17*

## READING PLAN

| | |
|---:|:---:|
| Day 1: | 1 Chronicles 27-29 |
| Day 2: | 2 Chronicles 1-4 |
| Day 3: | 2 Chronicles 5-7 |
| Day 4: | 2 Chronicles 8-11 |
| Day 5: | 2 Chronicles 12-16 |
| Day 6: | 2 Chronicles 17-20 |
| Day 7: | Rest Day/Catch Up |

## Faith in Action

Take a moment to pray and give the battle to the Lord that you need to surrender to Him. Let Him fight for you.

Week 19    Date: _____

# *Journal Questions*

1. Re-read Solomin's prayer in 2 Chronicles 1:7-12. Reflect on things in your own life where you may be asking God the wrong question.

2. What battles are you fighting right now that belong to the Lord?

3. We are told to pray, humble ourselves, and turn from our wicked ways. Is there any one of these that you have knowingly failed to do? What areas in your life can you humble yourself?

4. The Queen of Sheba "saw the wisdom of Solomon." (2 Chronicles 9:3) What do you think she saw?

# Week 19
# Reflection & Notes

# Gratitude

# Inspiration

It was a bright and sunny day in June 2015, when we headed off on a weekend family trip to Elitch Gardens in Denver. While having fun on a water slide ride, I was bounced off the mat I was laying on. Didn't seem like a big deal at that moment, but shortly after I started to feel a sharp pain in my back. In the following days and weeks, it went from being a small, inconsistent pain, to a nagging pain that began to go down my right leg.

Within a few weeks, I wasn't able to sit comfortably or sleep well. It got to the point that when we had friends over, I would rarely sit down because of the pain. I started to go to a chiropractor three times a week, but sadly it did not help at all. I tried a sports therapist, which did help momentarily, but the pain would always return. Out of frustration, I even tried cortisone injections, and still got no relief. The pain continued.

Three years later, I got the opportunity to visit the doctor who had saved my leg when it was crushed in a farm accident when I was 14 years old. I was grateful to see him for my back and hoped he would have some solutions for the pain. He determined I had a herniated disc between L4 and L5. He explained it like this, "Imagine taking a jelly filled donut and squeezing the jelly out. You can never properly get the jelly back in again." He suggested I would need to undergo surgery to restore it. We made plans to do surgery in the spring of 2018.

In the meantime, we went to a prayer and fasting event at our church. While we were there the pastor said, "We will be praying for healing tonight." As soon as he said that, something lit up inside of me and I knew it was for me!

The night took a different turn and we ended up spending a lot of time praying for marriages and closed the night without praying for any healing. I was a little disappointed because I had felt that there was healing for me.

On the second night, as soon as the pastor said, "let's pray for healing." I bolted up and was the first one up at the altar. I didn't want to miss my chance! I felt hands being placed on my shoulders and I heard someone praying over my back. My back started to get extremely hot and I started wondering, "Why did they put a hot pack on my back? That's weird!" Then, at that moment it hit me, "This is happening, this is really happening! This is happening to me!" The pain got so intense I had to go on my knees. I could literally feel my back and spine getting longer. The only way I can explain what happened is "the jelly went back in the donut."

For a few days after it happened, I was doubtful. I kept expecting the pain to come back. I was raised not believing in miracles and I had never experienced anything like that. It was all very new and unexpected. I didn't really tell anyone what had happened for the first few days, even though I was immediately able to sit, bend over and I was able to sleep all night, with absolutely no pain, for the first time in years.

Finally, it really truly hit me that I had been completely healed, and the pain wasn't ever coming back. I have been completely pain free for over four years now. God is still in the business of healing people!

*~Ben Miller*

# Week 20

*"And every work that he undertook in the service of the house of God and in accordance with the law and the commandments, seeking his God, he did with all his heart, and prospered."*
*~2 Chronicles 31:21*

## READING PLAN

| | |
|---|---|
| Day 1: | 2 Chronicles 21-23 |
| Day 2: | 2 Chronicles 24-26 |
| Day 3: | 2 Chronicles 27-29 |
| Day 4: | 2 Chronicles 30-32 |
| Day 5: | 2 Chronicles 33-36 |
| Day 6: | Ezra 1-4 |
| Day 7: | Rest Day/Catch Up |

## Faith in Action

Write (or text) someone in your life a "thank you" note telling them you're grateful for them.

Week 20     Date: _____

## *Journal Questions*

1. If there was one thing you could ask God to restore for you personally, what would that be? Why?

2. What's something that stood out to you in the scripture reading this week? What's something you struggled to understand? Pray and ask God to help you have a deeper understanding.

3. King Ahab had poor counselors speaking into his life that led him astray from God *(2 Chronicles 22:2-5.)* Who are you allowing to speak into your life, or give you counsel? Does it line up with the Word of God?

4. God calls us to be a "holy" or "set apart" people. Reading through Ezra, is there anything in your life that God may be asking you to shift away from to set yourself apart?

# Week 20
## Reflection & Notes

## Gratitude

# Inspiration

In the early morning hours of November 22, 2015, my company responded to our second structural fire in under twenty four hours. I was a firefighter for 28.5 years at that point and the company captain.

We knocked down the fire inside the house in record time but there was still a fire in the attic, so I ordered a crew to extinguish it. A little while later I climbed up to the attic to verify the status and quickly realized it was still burning. I was alone when the ceiling collapsed in its entirety. I fell head first nine feet down, landing on the top of my head.

I was instantly paralyzed. Awake and fully conscious, I screamed "Help me! Help me!" but words never left my mind because I could not breathe. I lay there on my side, unable to move, as I watched firemen's boots walking around me.

One of the firemen finally looked down and knew something was wrong. He acted quickly to secure my spine and get it in line. Reaching down, he grabbed my head and turned it just enough to relieve some of the pressure on my spinal cord allowing me to breathe. I was running out of air, so the crew moved quickly to pull off my mask and helmet. As they worked to remove my air pack I screamed "No!" and informed them that my neck was broken. A little feeling returned to my arms and I was able to move slightly. I begged for my family, wanting to hug them. I knew once they moved me, I would become completely paralyzed. "Captain, we can't bring your family into a burning building."

At the hospital an ER doctor read my MRI and remarked, "I don't know how you are alive." My neck was broken along with other vertebrae in my back. As they wheeled me off to emergency surgery, I reassured my daughter I would be fine, but I knew the reality—I would either be paralyzed from the neck down or die on the operating table.

There are only three to four thousand people in my small community but word of my accident got out quickly. An estimated one million people around the country prayed for me. I could feel their prayers as I woke up from surgery moving my hands and feet.

The surgeon who had prayed with me and my family before whisking me off to surgery came into my room and exclaimed, "There is no medical reason you are alive. I have done this for three decades and there is absolutely no reason your spinal cord did not snap. I have never seen one that bad that didn't snap."

Since then, every single doctor that has examined my x-rays tells me the best case scenario is that I should have been paralyzed from the neck down, breathing out of my throat. However, I have always known God had something bigger and better for me. This accident ended my firefighting career but I was promoted to Training Officer, then Operations Fire Chief. As the #2 Fire Chief, I was able to make beneficial changes that forever altered the lives of our men. My number one goal was to protect and take care of them. I thought that was my highest calling until I became a coach and walked on to the speaking stage. I believe God saved me for a greater purpose and I am pursuing it the way I once ran toward fire.

God pulled me out of the flames and then healed me. I still live with pain, but that pain reminds me that I'm alive. They said "there is no medical reason" and there is not... There is a divine reason that I survived that fall.

~Todd Sanford

# Week 21

"Then he said to them, 'Go your way. Eat the fat and drink sweet wine and send portions to anyone who has nothing ready, for this day is holy to our Lord. And do not be grieved, for the joy of the Lord is your strength.'" ~ *Nehemiah 8:10*

## READING PLAN

| | |
|---|---|
| Day 1: | Ezra 5-7 |
| Day 2: | Ezra 8-10 |
| Day 3: | Nehemiah 1-4 |
| Day 4: | Nehemiah 5-7 |
| Day 5: | Nehemiah 8-10 |
| Day 6: | Nehemiah 11-13 |
| Day 7: | Rest Day/Catch Up |

## Faith in Action

Do you have a testimony to share about how God brought you through a trial, to refine you in Him or to bring you to Him? Write out your testimony so you are prepared to share it as He leads you.

Week 21    Date: _____

## Journal Questions

1. In Hebrew, Nehemiah means "God comforts." How is that name relatable to what you read this week? How has He comforted you in your life?

2. Has there ever been a time in your life when you wanted to give up? How did you continue forward?

3. God calls Ezra to restore the temple before Nehemiah restores the city. What is the significance of this order and how can you apply it in your own life?

4. Why was the Lord so upset with the people who married foreign wives? How can we apply this to our lives today?

# Week 21
# Reflection & Notes

# Gratitude

# INSPIRATION

Years ago, I was diagnosed with anxiety, depression, panic disorder, severe PTSD, and suffered through daily seizures. It was a very miserable time in my life. Through Biblical forgiveness work, I was able to become completely free from all of it for four years. I was convinced it was gone for good.

Then, in 2019, I lost everything. I lost a pregnancy. I lost the company I had built. I lost my childhood dream I'd worked for. I ended up back in severe depression, with PTSD, and seizures again. Just like the first time, I thought it would all go away, but it didn't.

Fifteen months went by quickly. My life shifted. Our family moved fulltime into an RV and began traveling. I had less stress in my life. I was happy and fulfilled, yet I was still suffering from seizures. I finally went to the doctor where they ran countless tests, but didn't find answers. Eventually, a neurologist officially diagnosed me with epilepsy. I was crushed! I had been in denial that anything was wrong with me. Even though having seizures had become so normal that my kids didn't flinch anymore when I had them.

I decided to not be defined by my diagnosis. I had overcome seizures before, and I believed this time God would heal me for His glory. I would tell people, "A doctor diagnosed me with epilepsy, but God is going to heal me. I don't know where or when, but I know He is!"

Yet, when that day came, I still walked in denial. Even though I had witnessed a friend be miraculously healed out of a wheelchair, somehow a part of me still doubted that miracles were real.

In March of 2022, I was miraculously healed at a business training event. There was a pastor, named Benny Perez, on stage healing people in the crowd. He began saying, "There is somebody here having issues with your brain..." As he spoke, I remember thinking to myself, "That sounds like it could be me," while looking over the crowd and wondering why no one was raising their hand. Then I heard the Holy Spirit whisper, "No one is raising their hand because it's YOU he is talking about!"

At that moment, I screamed in my head, "Noooooooo!" and began to argue with God that it couldn't possibly be me! My body suddenly began to burn like it was on fire, and a force beyond my control began to propel my body to the stage. When I got there, Pastor Benny spoke to me for a minute, and then he declared, "As quickly as it came, it's leaving even quicker now!" And then I fell to the ground...not once...not twice...but three times! As I sat up on the floor, I felt hot, dazed, and confused. Yet... I knew I was healed!

What was also amazing, is that earlier that day, I had posted on Facebook that I was looking for stories of miraculous healing for my next Bible Study Journal I was creating. I never dreamed God wanted me to be one of those stories!

It has been almost two years now and I have been seizure free, which still is incredible to me. Honestly, I still have moments of doubt about my healing. When someone is healed out of a wheelchair, you can see it. You can see them walk again. I can't show people evidence that I have been healed from seizures. I simply don't have them anymore.

I think that is why God wanted me to share my story with you. To let you know it's okay if you have doubt. Just don't stay there! I almost let doubt steal away my moment of healing. Don't miss your moment. Miracles are everywhere, and I believe God has one waiting for you!

*~Summer Dey*

# Week 22

"For if you keep silent at this time, relief and deliverance will rise for the Jews from another place, but you and your father's house will perish. And who knows whether you have not come to the kingdom for such a time as this?" ~*Esther 4:14*

## READING PLAN

| | |
|---:|---:|
| Day 1: | Esther 1-3 |
| Day 2: | Esther 4-6 |
| Day 3: | Esther 7-10 |
| Day 4: | Job 1-3 |
| Day 5: | Job 4-8 |
| Day 6: | Job 9-13 |
| Day 7: | Rest Day/Catch Up |

## Faith in Action

Is there something that has been a huge distraction for you? Perhaps it has even been distracting you from God. Take time to finish that task this week, remove it, or give yourself a time limit so you can move forward.

Week 22     Date: _____

## *Journal Questions*

1. In Ester chapter 2, Mordecai does the right thing but he is not immediately rewarded for it. Have there been times in your life where you did the right thing even though nobody seemed to notice? Reflect in light of this story.

2. God used Esther to protect His people. She had to choose to not stay silent and to go against her society, culture, and the king's policy, yet she found favor. Has there been a time when you needed to speak up or do something hard that may have been contrary to the world, yet He granted you favor? How can you be ready if He asks you to do something like that in the future?

3. Job was stripped away from all his earthly possessions and even suffered physical ailments. If you were in Job's shoes, how would you feel or react? How can we still turn to God and rely on Him in our toughest moments?

4. Does it seem like either party is listening to the other in the conversation between Job and his friends? Do you tend to intently listen to others when they speak or do you hear just enough to quickly respond and interject your own opinion? How can you become a better listener?

## Week 22
## Reflection & Notes

## Gratitude

# INSPIRATION

Ten years ago, I found myself in a lot of pain along with onset migraines that I had never experienced. It was absolutely debilitating. I could not work, or do anything with my children. It affected my relationship with them and it affected my social and married life too.

Previously, I suffered the aches and pains left over from my military experience but this was different. I experience strange burning sensations in my hands and feet and constant, intense body aches. My doctors had no answers, stillI continued on. I ran my own cleaning business. At the end of the day I would pull up in my driveway, sit, and cry because the pain was so raw and unrelenting.

After going to several doctors, I was finally given a diagnosis: Arnold Chiari malformation. An MRI revealed that my brain was sitting on the back of my skull. To relieve the pain, I would need to have decompression surgery. I found out the left side of my body was in atrophy, which answered so many questions. I walked out in tears utterly devastated. I thought to myself, "I am only thirty-five years old. There is no way God is going to have me live like this! Are you kidding?" As I pondered my future, I felt defeated. I asked myself, "What does this look like as I get older? Do I really have to live with this condition that affects every aspect of my life?"

I believed prayer would normally get me out of a situation, but this was a low blow. I desperately sought relief and made an appointment with a neurosurgeon. One Friday, I navigated the hour drive to my appointment, only for it to be canceled five minutes from the office. I sighed heavily, rescheduled for Monday, and turned back toward home.

Doped up on medication, that Sunday I went to church, listening from the back of the church and not really present. Suddenly, the pastor stopped the service and called me up. "We need to intercede and pray for you." I knew in that moment relief was coming as the entire church interceded for me. I realized God cared enough to stop an entire service just for me.

I was instantly healed in that service. I felt a jolt of electricity from the top of my head to the soles of my feet. My pastor shared a revelation from God that my surgeon would say, "Why are you here? There is nothing wrong with you. You don't need surgery."

I was determined to see the neurosurgeon. I didn't feel the burning and the pain was gone. I asked my husband to come with me because I was expecting a miracle. We sat in the waiting room, only to be told we needed to reschedule once again.

I knew I needed to see the doctor because what was spoken over me had to come to pass. The doctor needed to ask me why I was there. We insisted on waiting for him until he finally called me in. "Well why are you here? I am looking at the x-rays and they are normal. You don't have Arnold Chiari malformation."

I asked, "Are you sure you are looking at my x-rays?" He pointed to the slides with my name at the top and the abnormal formation was gone! I asked about my atrophy so he tested my muscles and the degeneration was no longer present. God had healed me completely!

Unless you experience God for yourself, even on a small scale, you really don't understand what He can do. He can move mountains. He can restore all things. He can move the hearts of kings and evil doers and I am here to tell you, there is a trickle effect to miracles.

~Raquel Foreman

# Week 23

"And he said to man, 'Behold, the fear of the Lord, that is wisdom, and to turn away from evil is understanding.'" ~*Job 28:28*

## READING PLAN

| | |
|---|---|
| Day 1: | Job 14-18 |
| Day 2: | Job 19-22 |
| Day 3: | Job 23-27 |
| Day 4: | Job 28-31 |
| Day 5: | Job 32-35 |
| Day 6: | Job 36-38 |
| Day 7: | Rest Day/Catch Up |

## Faith in Action

Take action to bring a person solace this week by sending a note of encouragement, volunteering to babysit, or paying for lunch, etc

Week 23      Date: _____

## *Journal Questions*

1. It seems as if God was silent during Job's trials. Job doesn't hear from God again until the end when he repents and God lifts him up. Is there a time when God has felt silent? How have you dealt with that?

2. Job was having back and forth conversations with his friends. They seemed to have different views and opinions. What unshakeable convictions do you have about God that no one can change your mind on?

3. What can you glean from the story of Job and learn in moments of silence from God?

4. In Job 38, God speaks to Job again. What do you learn about God, His nature and character in these verses?

# Week 23
## Reflection & Notes

## Gratitude

# Inspiration

June 26, 1971, I was taken ill with what they thought was heatstroke. I had been complaining of terrible headaches, had a fever of 106, and was talking out of my mind. Two days later, when my aunt and grandma were visiting, they noticed I was unresponsive. My mom was shocked. She thought I was just sleeping. They immediately rushed me to Saint Francis Hospital. By this point, I was already in a coma. I was thrashing uncontrollably as they tried to work on me. My mom said she began to repeat to me, "Jesus, Jesus, Jesus!" and I calmed down enough for them to do what they needed to.

It was later determined I had Encephalitis and Spinal Meningitis. They sent a priest in to give me my last rights. Doctors told my parents I had less than 8 hours to live, and if by any chance I did live, I would probably be a vegetable for the rest of my life.

For three days straight, I screamed nonstop. I had to be tied completely to the bed from my head to my feet because of the constant thrashing. A nurse had to hold something in my mouth to keep me from swallowing my tongue. My family began to get countless people around the world to pray for a miracle. They were very close friends with Oral Roberts at the time, and he stopped mid-sermon, in front of 3,000 people to pray for me.

Then, as quickly as it started, I suddenly stopped thrashing after three days in a coma. When I woke up, I can remember trying to move. I tried to talk, but couldn't. I kept hearing the beeping noises, and voices calmly repeating my name, "Todd, Todd, Todd, it's alright, Todd, Todd, Todd."

The nurse started hollering for help and people ran in all around the bed. Everyone was talking and everything was white. My mind was racing, thinking it was a dream. I thought to myself, "Am I dead? Where am I? Who are these people?" They checked my vitals, and I kept trying to talk. I remember feeling scared. And I kept hearing those calm voices saying, "Todd, Todd, Todd." When they finally removed the tube out of my mouth, I started talking. They were amazed. They started asking me all kinds of questions. They removed all of my restraints.

At this point, I could see three women at the foot of my bed; two caucasian women with an African American woman in the middle. They were beautiful and were wearing all white. They said, "Todd, Todd, Todd," and then all the other questions started again. They were crazy questions, I thought.

My mom and dad were outside the door to my room putting on what looked like white robes, so I still thought I was still dreaming. It turns out they were putting on sanitary gowns.

After two more spinal taps, numerous tests, countless questions and visits from several more doctors, I was finally released. The doctors told my parents it was a miracle that only God could have done! I had gone from being given less than 8 hours to live, to walking out the door, in just three weeks.

At the time, I was the youngest person to survive with the strains of encephalitis and spinal meningitis that I had. It was especially miraculous that I endured no side effects or complications of any type as well.

Later, when I asked who the three women were at the foot of my bed when I woke up out of a coma, no one could tell me. I never saw them again after that brief encounter. I described them to everyone and none of them saw them, but me. I now know Jesus sent them, and know they were my Guardian Angels.

*~Todd Jones*

# Week 24

"And those who tknow your name put their trust in you, for you, O Lord, have not forsaken those who seek you." ~*Psalm 9:10*

## READING PLAN

| | |
|---|---|
| Day 1: | Job 39-42 |
| Day 2: | Psalms 1-8 |
| Day 3: | Psalms 9-16 |
| Day 4: | Psalms 17-19 |
| Day 5: | Psalms 20-25 |
| Day 6: | Psalms 26-31 |
| Day 7: | Rest Day/Catch Up |

## Faith in Action

Meditate on His goodness as we wade into Psalms. The Psalms are meant for praise and worship. Find a song that sings one of the Psalms and listen to it throughout the week.

Week 24    Date: _____

# *Journal Questions*

1. We end the book of Job and see his trials and then how God blessed him even greater in the latter days of his life. Is there a time in your life where you went through a hard time and then came out better off? Or if you are currently in a hard time, how can Job's story give you hope?

2. King David walked through many trials in his lifetime, but through it all he chose to praise God. What are ways you can praise God even in the hard times?

3. In chapter 19 the Psalmist concludes by saying, "May the words of my mouth and the meditation of my heart be pleasing to You." Reflect on the meditation of your heart. Is it pleasing to Him?

4. Psalm 20:4 states, "May He grant you your heart's desire and fulfill all your plans." What are your plans and desires? Do they line up with God's heart and character as we see in the Scriptures?

# Week 24
## Reflection & Notes

## Gratitude

# Inspiration

My husband and I both have a history of febrile seizures, a condition that causes high fevers leading to a seizure lasting for several minutes. When we had our first biological daughter together we were warned our children would have a heightened risk of seizures.

When our second biological child Memphis was born, I knew there was something different and special about her. When she was just four months old her head began to tilt to one side, but doctors assured me everything was normal. At thirteen months she was still not speaking and I was extremely worried. I took her back to a pediatrician who diagnosed her with torticollis. Her sternum calcoid muscle was shorter on one side, causing her head to tilt. I brought up my concerns about her lack of speech but they excused it as the result of her older siblings speaking for her.

Rejecting that diagnosis, they connected me with BabyNet and Memphis was given an early interventionist. When the Early Interventionist interviewed us, Memphis had a meltdown qualifying her for the program. They ran tests but the speech pathologist could find no reason why she was not speaking. I was told her receptive language was off the charts and they were sure she didn't have autism.

We immediately started physical therapy for her neck. All the therapists remarked how smart she was. When Memphis was two, she was prescribed speech therapy, but by three years old she had still made no progress and aged out of the program. At her elementary school a speech pathologist diagnosed her with congenital apraxia. I was told she may never speak, however we continued with speech therapy because I knew it could only help.

I will never forget that April when Memphis was three and a half. We were leaving the beach and as I dressed her I discovered she was warm. Ever concerned about febrile seizures in my babies I began to rush her home.

We got home and I ripped out a thermometer - 102.6°! A fever of 103° meant a high risk of seizure. I quickly ran a bath and within minutes her eyes glazed over and she was gone. I looked at my baby who appeared in a zombie state and screamed her name. She threw up but wasn't conscious so I scooped her out of the bath and thrust my finger in her mouth to sweep out the vomit. She bit down on my finger, chewing down on my nail bed. I knew what febrile seizures looked like, this looked like a demonic possession.

My sixteen year old called 911 as I prayed the Lord's prayer repeatedly over her while pounding on her back to wake her up. I screamed to the Lord, "Don't take her from me! Don't do this to me! I love her so much." She finally let go of my nail-bed, and fell back lifeless. I held her thinking she had died. As I prayed, she opened her eyes and looked at me almost as if nothing had happened.

When we had her tested afterwards and her EEG came back normal, her pediatrician was convinced a febrile seizure had occurred. However, I knew better.

Two weeks later, Memphis abruptly started talking to us in complete sentences. Her speech pathologists were dumbfounded. They rescinded their diagnosis and discharged her from speech therapy. Memphis is twelve now. We never complain and ask her to stop when she talks too much!

I know that day when I prayed over her, God intervened and gave us a miracle. The enemy came and attacked, but God redeemed.

~Erin Mansour

# Week 25

"Create in me a clean heart, O God, and renew a right spirit within me." ~*Psalm 51:10*

## READING PLAN

| | |
|---|---|
| Day 1: | Psalms 32-35 |
| Day 2: | Psalms 36-40 |
| Day 3: | Psalms 41-46 |
| Day 4: | Psalms 47-52 |
| Day 5: | Psalms 53-58 |
| Day 6: | Psalms 59-66 |
| Day 7: | Rest Day/Catch Up |

## Faith in Action

Pray and ask God to show you the goodness in His Word as you read the Psalms. We are called to meditate on His Word day and night. .

Week 25      Date: _____

# Journal Questions

1. Psalm 50 speaks to "my people" and "the wicked." Compare and contrast what God says to His people versus those who walk in wickedness?

2. God does not promise us an easy life but rather to always be with us, to sustain us, to comfort us, and that the end with Him is better than any riches of the earth. How can you lean in more and trust Him with your life?

3. David talks about fearing God often in the Psalms. What does it mean to "fear God"?

4. Psalm 66:10 says that "God has proved us and refined us as silver." What does it mean to be refined? Do you have an example from your life?

# Week 25
## Reflection & Notes

## Gratitude

# INSPIRATION

As a fourth-generation preacher, I learned at a young age to listen to God. I accepted Christ and received the gift of tongues at the age of six. I was accepted to West Point Military Academy, but God told me he wanted me to preach, so I went to Bible College. While attending South Eastern University and Oral Roberts University doors quickly opened revealing His plan for my life.

I was a pilot for many years, flying a small twin engine plane. One evening as I flew my plane home from a meeting, the instruments on my plane suddenly went out. I immediately radioed the control tower to report the malfunction. Just then, the right engine went out, and I knew I was in trouble. The scripture that came to me at that moment was *"my God is an ever-present help in times of trouble."* [Psalm 46:1]

My plane descended through a dark thunderstorm, and I crashed into a wooded area filled with thick pine trees. My foot and nose were torn off, my hip was crushed, ribs broken, and I was drowning in my own blood. As I lay there with a tree across my chest, I heard demons revel around me, "We got him. We got Charlie Fowler! He won't be preaching anymore revivals. We've stopped him from building churches and schools!" But the delight of these evil spirits was premature. Instantly, the Holy Spirit came down upon me as I prayed, "I shall not die, but live, and declare the works of the Lord." [Psalm 118:17]

That night many people searched the woods for my wrecked plane. The next morning a deputy sheriff, who was a part of the search team, spotted a Hunter parked on the side of the road and asked if he knew where my plane went down. Miraculously, the Hunter directed the deputy sheriff directly to my location and he found me barely holding onto life, covered in gasoline. He radioed the rescue helicopter, and they were able to reach me. With the rescue team struggling to free me from the weight of the pine tree that was lying on my chest, I felt the Hunter next to my head. Without touching me, the Hunter said, "My God, My God, My God,".... By the third time, the tree released its grip and freed me. That local deputy sheriff gave his life to the Lord instantly the moment he realized that "Hunter" was an angel sent by God to save my life.

The flight surgeon on the rescue team warned I would not survive the flight to the hospital. Laying on the gurney, I opened my eyes and professed "I shall not die, but live!" In the hospital, I spent weeks enduring multiple surgeries. While I had survived the plane crash, doctors determined I would never stand or walk again.

After seven weeks, I was permitted to return home to continue recuperating. Bound to a wheelchair, more weeks passed, and despair grew into depression.

During a Tuesday Night Bible Study, while preaching on Faith, I asked God, "How can I preach that you are a God who heals while I sit in this wheelchair?" God answered through His Word, Hebrews 11:1 - *"Now Faith!"*

Believing His Word, I told the congregation if they believed I was going to be healed tonight to stand up and worship the Lord. I said, "By His Stripes we are healed, and we were healed, so I am healed," and I jumped out of my wheelchair and started to walk! I was healed by the power of God. Since then, I've preached to thousands of people all over the world. I'm alive today because of the power of The Word of God. There is power in His Word.

*~Dr. Charlie Fowler, Author of "I Shall Not Die But Live," www.AwakeTheWorld.org*

# Week 26

"He who dwells in the shelter of the Most High will abide in the shadow of the Almighty. I will say to the Lord, 'My refuge and my fortress, my God, in whom I trust.'" ~*Psalm 91:1-2*

## READING PLAN

Day 1:         Psalms 67-69
Day 2:         Psalms 70-74
Day 3:         Psalms 75-79
Day 4:         Psalms 80-87
Day 5:         Psalms 88-93
Day 6:         Psalms 94-102
Day 7:         Rest Day/Catch Up

## Faith in Action

Pick one of the Psalms you read this week, write it out by hand and put it up where you can see it daily.

Week 26      Date: _____

# Journal Questions

1. Many of the Psalms mention "idols" or "other gods." Idols often can be a figure or statue that people worship, however it can also be anything that we raise up above God, such as money, work, exercise, ourselves, family, or friendships. What idols do you struggle with in your life??

2. What are some promises that you enjoyed reading about in the Psalms this week?

3. Psalm 91:4 says, "God is our shield and protector." How has He protected you in your life?

4. Righteousness is mentioned often in the scriptures. What is righteousness according to the Bible?

# Week 26
## Reflection & Notes

## Gratitude

# Inspiration

My whole life changed when the doctor said, "I'm sorry, but there is nothing that can be done about your nerve damage. You will not regain the abilities in your legs." Fear consumed me while sitting there in my wheelchair, until I heard a voice say, "But, you serve a God who heals!" The second I agreed with that statement, the fear completely left.

One day, a friend came over to lay hands on me, and as she prayed she said, "I keep seeing you dancing in a flower field." Her vision gave me hope.

Months passed by. I stumbled online upon a picture of a woman dancing in a flower field. It was a women's retreat that was happening in the three days. When I called the number they said, "We actually had a cancellation today and have one spot!"

At the retreat, the pastor came over to me in my walker and asked, "How did you hear about us?" I heard a powerful voice yell in my mind, "Do not tell them that you are here to be healed because when you are not, everyone's faith will be on the line!" I fought against the fear and yelled out, "I am here to be healed and I am supposed to dance in that flower field!" The whole room went crazy yelling, "Amen! Yes Lord! Heal her Lord!"

A bit later, a young lady prayed for me and said, "Oh honey, the Lord wants you to deal with this unforgiveness." Another woman prayed and cried because she said she saw a seven-year-old boy with dark hair who had a spirit of murder and suicide on him. I immediately knew she was talking about my son. He talked about those things all the time. I asked where the spirit came from? She replied, "His name sake?" I asked her how to get rid of it. She said, "You just ask Jesus. It's His will to set your son free." I asked the Lord to heal my baby and immediately I could feel the heaviness come off of me. I knew healing happened at that moment for my son. The other woman asked, "Who do you need to forgive?" I replied, "I need to forgive my father, who committed suicide when I was pregnant with my son, whom I named him after." As soon as I forgave my father, peace overwhelmed me.

At midnight, the pastor announced it was time to leave the room. I immediately told the Lord, "Your Word says You will not put your servant to shame. Please do not allow me to leave without dancing in that flower field." Just then, a little girl walked up to me and asked if she could pray for me. I knew this would be the final breakthrough. She said, "Jesus will you heal her so she can go back and show the doctors that Jesus still heals in Jesus name, amen!" Something happened at that moment! I asked Jesus, "I've been asking You all day to let me run to You. Will you just let me run to You?" I immediately felt an alignment in my hips and my back. I moved the walker to the side. I lifted one leg and it was light. I lifted the next leg and it was light! I began to run and kept running while screaming, "THANK YOU, JESUS!"

The Lord healed me that day! When I got home to share what Lord had done with my family, my seven-year-old son came over and sat next to me. He did not even look the same. There was this new found peace in his eyes. He said to me, "Jesus wants me to tell you that my heart is happy now." That child had been transformed, which was another beautiful miracle! And God wasn't finished with His miracles for our family. I gave birth to a baby girl on the one year anniversary date of my healing because the Lord wanted me to always remember and celebrate what He did that day!

~Jennifer Loza

# Week 27

"I lift up my eyes to the hills. From where does my help come? My help comes from the Lord, who made heaven and earth."
~Psalm 121:1-2

## READING PLAN

| | |
|---|---|
| Day 1: | Psalms 103-106 |
| Day 2: | Psalms 107-109 |
| Day 3: | Psalms 110-118 |
| Day 4: | Psalms 119 |
| Day 5: | Psalms 120-126 |
| Day 6: | Psalms 127-136 |
| Day 7: | Rest Day/Catch Up |

## Faith in Action

Congratulations! You are halfway through reading the Bible! Spend an extra 20 minutes this week journaling about what God is teaching you through your scripture readings.

Week 27     Date: _____

# Journal Questions

1. A great way to praise God in times of trouble is to recount all the blessings and things He has already done for us. What prayers has the Lord already answered? What are some things He has already done for you, specifically?

2. Several Psalms reveal a prophetic promise of the coming Messiah. What do we learn about Jesus, our Messiah, in Psalm 110?

3. In reading through the Psalms, what does love look like to God? How does King David show God love, and how does God show love to him, and us?

4. What does it look like to trust God, to truly trust Him? What would look different in your life if you trusted Him fully? How can your actions and words reflect that you trust Him?

# Week 27
## Reflection & Notes

## Gratitude

# Inspiration

After 57 hours of labor, our little king, David Vicente Del Rio, was born into this world at 12:10 pm on July 8, 2023. His birth was an incredible experience raising new levels of awareness and adventure. The supernatural is real but so is the demonic. Thank God I know my authority in Him and the difference. If we aren't tapped into heightened awareness, our experiences can be very deceiving.

I am 41 years old and had two cesareans before. This VBAC (vaginal birth after cesarean) was a heightened concern. To complicate things, David was in the occiput posterior position known as "sunny side up."

When my entourage and I arrived for his birth, it was clear my midwife was already tired, as she had done a delivery that morning. I asked if she believed I could do this, as she was the expert. She responded, "You know the baby is healthy, there's a good heartbeat, as long as you're willing to keep trudging along, I will." My doula, Chandra, jumped in, "You look into my eyes... If anyone can do this it is you." My midwife chimed in, "But also the baby is sunny side up, so that is going to make it way harder." If I had not learned to put my thoughts under submission, I would have given pause but I immediately answered, "Good thing God created me to do hard things!"

I was very purposeful about not allowing negative thoughts to stay in my mind. When a doubt or fear crept in, I rejected them with the potent statement, "Those are not my thoughts!" I don't know what I'm doing, but God does. The truth is, I didn't need my midwife's assurance. I didn't even contact her until I was in my 35th week and the only reason I did was for the sake of my husband, my mother, and Chandra, who wasn't comfortable being the expert.

God guided me every minute of the journey. He helped me turn inward and step into another dimension with Him. For example, the times my mom felt bad for me working so hard and not having the baby out, I was off in the supernatural doing back strokes in the ocean with God not feeling an ounce of pain. I thought it was 20 minutes, but I now know it was more like five to six hours. I floated and dove deep underwater with the Lord during the majority of my most impactful labor. At times my birthing team exclaimed "this is amazing progress, push just like that Brandi" yet I felt like I was merely floating, doing nothing but smiling and breathing.

The enemy tries to be clever with words like "concerns." That is a root of doubt and unbelief which is not of God. God is more than able. Who am I to deny what the Lord can do? I overcame every concern that was being thrown my way. I pressed into Holy Spirit and submitted to Him. If He guided me in another direction, I would surrender.

My contractions seemed to cease. After only two contractions in ninety minutes, my midwife suggested maybdone my body was telling us something. I understood her reasoning so I covered my face and pressed into God. I heard "No." Which meant don't go to the hospital.

Chandra got me to my feet while my cousin started the music. A contraction! The toilet was the closest place to sit and that was the position! I cried out to Heavenly Father, went for it, and David crowned. David's final release happened so fast that I was in awe. Being in my own bed with my family minutes after delivery made every second worth it. I did it. God did it through me. He truly does get all the glory.

*~Brandi Del Rio*

# Week 28

"The fear of the Lord is the beginning of knowledge, but fools despise wisdom and instruction." ~*Proverbs 1:7*

## READING PLAN

| | |
|---:|---:|
| Day 1: | Psalms 137-143 |
| Day 2: | Psalms 144-150 |
| Day 3: | Proverbs 1-4 |
| Day 4: | Proverbs 5-7 |
| Day 5: | Proverbs 8-11 |
| Day 6: | Proverbs 12-15 |
| Day 7: | Rest Day/Catch Up |

## Faith in Action

Make a list of those who may need your forgiveness and ask God to walk you through forgiving them.

Week 28        Date: _____

## Journal Questions

1. What is wisdom according to Scripture? What are some differences between wisdom from God and wisdom from the world?

2. As believers, how do we stray from evil and stay in the ways of the Lord? What are some things God hates, and seem unwise, that we are warned to stay away from in Proverbs?

3. What is pride in God's eyes? What is humility?

4. While reading this week, what thoughts came up that you need to change or get rid of so that they don't become a stumbling block, or lead to foolishness? Ask for forgiveness, pray, and seek Him on how to grow in wisdom.

# Week 28
# Reflection & Notes

# Gratitude

# Inspiration

I was a young, new believer and at twenty-one years old, my husband and I moved to Washington state. My life before God had left me without hope and my confidence as a young believer was still in its infancy.

I was not a mother and although I was in a church group with a lot of mothers, I didn't know if I ever wanted to be a mom. I began looking for a job in our new town. I had a marketing degree with a minor in art, but I honestly felt called to work at Starbucks as a barista.

I kept Tuesdays clear for a Bible study fellowship group I belonged to, but one particular Tuesday I agreed to cover someone's shift following my Bible study. At that meeting we were instructed to be faithful wherever God places us because He has us where He wants us in that given moment. That space is our sacred ministry.

I went to work bothered by this thought. I wasn't in ministry, I was "just" a barista. While I felt positive God called me to that position, I didn't see any Godly purpose.

As I put on my apron in the backroom, I began ruminating over my imagined insufficiencies. "I'm only a barista. How can God use me? I have a degree and I am artistic, but I don't know why or how God would use me."

Feeling distraught I reminded myself I was there for the customer, and to put on a smile and be present for them. I don't remember the door opening but all of a sudden there was a customer walking toward me with his eyes locked on mine as if he were there to see me.

"Hi, your smile is radiant!" were the first words out of his mouth. He continued to compliment me, pouring kind affirmations into me. He told me I glowed and spoke about a light around me. "You are glorious, the brightest thing here." My coworker rolled his eyes, but the man's non-stop compliments weren't said in a weird or creepy way. As I handed him his cup of coffee he asked, "You have a faith about you don't you?"

"Yes," I smiled. "I can tell," he winked. He instructed me to keep my smile and my glow. I turned to my coworker and said, "Ryan did you hear that?" He looked at me blankly, "What?" he mumbled.

I turned back to the man but he was gone. No bell announced his departure, and no bell sounded when he arrived, although the bell on the glass door was quite loud as I ran out to search for him in the parking lot. He wasn't in the bathrooms either. He never left, he never came, but he answered all of the questions I was pondering.

"Why am I here? What am I doing? Is my purpose even worth it? Does God even care what I'm up to?" At that point I knew the answer and I embraced my calling at Starbucks. I became a bright light for people grabbing their morning coffee at 5 a.m. I was once told by a man that I saved his marriage because the advice I gave him helped them move forward and heal. I knew I was there for that purpose and thousands more as I lovingly scrawled names on each cup of coffee.

I draw from that experience whenever I question whether I am doing a good job at the various roles I find myself in. The angel in Starbucks told me that God called me to spread light and encouragement. He said to me, "Your radiance shines eternal glory." I want to honor my Lord by radiating His light to others wherever I go.

~Natasha Schuerman

# Week 29

"Death and life are in the power of the tongue, and those who love it will eat its fruits." ~*Proverbs 18:21*

## READING PLAN

| | |
|---:|---:|
| Day 1: | Proverbs 16-19 |
| Day 2: | Proverbs 20-23 |
| Day 3: | Proverbs 24-27 |
| Day 4: | Proverbs 28-31 |
| Day 5: | Ecclesiastes 1-4 |
| Day 6: | Ecclesiastes 5-8 |
| Day 7: | Rest Day/Catch Up |

## Faith in Action

Pray and ask God to help you become a God-fearing believer.

Week 29  Date: _____

# Journal Questions

1. God cares about what comes out of your mouth and how you control your tongue. Slander and gossip are sin in God's eyes. Are you guilty of this? What are steps you can take to change these habits?

2. You finished Proverbs this week. What Proverb stood out to you the most and you feel God used to speak to you? Why do you feel it spoke to you?

3. If you are man who is married, write out Proverbs 31:10-31 and pray this over your wife as a blessing. If you are a woman who is married, write this out and pray for God to refine you into a Proverbs 31 wife.

4. According to Ecclesiastes 3, everything has a time and season appointed by God. Recognizing the season you are in can give you clarity, focus, and the ability to prepare for the next season. What season are you in right now? What are ways you can be better prepared for it?

# Week 29
## Reflection & Notes

## Gratitude

# Inspiration

After surrendering my life to Christ at eighteen years old, I developed multiple female health problems. At first, I thought these were consequences from my life before Jesus. These problems left me wondering if I'd ever be able to live out my dream of becoming a mom. Throughout the following decade these problems escalated into chronic pain. This pain felt like fire was burning on the inside of me. Days were uncomfortable and nights were tormenting. My only option was to cling to Jesus and His promises. He became my everything and He helped me see these trials were my path to restoration and redemption.

Doctors could not figure out the root of the chronic pain and eventually diagnosed me with nerve pain. The only option for pain management was heavy nerve blockers also known as antidepressants. This medication lowered my pain to a level two, but left me fatigued all day long, even after sleeping ten hours a night. When most young adults are thriving in their twenties, I was undergoing my wilderness season learning to rely on Jesus for everything. Inner healing was my favorite pain remedy during this time, bringing me into a deep intimacy with Jesus as He healed the many wounds of my heart.

God also gave me the faith to believe I would have children, and a husband. He gave me their names to pray for them by faith, yes, even my future husband's name. Nine months after praying for my husband by name, he walked into the church I had been working at. All he had to do was introduce himself as "Anthony" and I knew he was the one I had been praying for. We got married a year later.

I quickly discovered my husband's faith was greater than mine. A few months into our marriage, he was determined to set me free from my infirmity and see me get off the terrible medication I was on. He led me in prayer and commanded an unclean spirit off of me. Immediately, I saw in the spirit a thorny bush unravel itself off my waist and slink away like a snake. I was shocked! Mainly because I didn't think I could have an evil spirit oppressing me since I was full of the Holy Spirit. I learned a good lesson that day.

He encouraged me to take a leap of faith and not take my meds that night. I followed his advice and by the next morning I was overcome by level nine pain. As I reached for my meds that night I heard the Holy Spirit prompt me to ask my husband first. I went to my husband and told him, "I'm taking my meds tonight!" He suggested we pray again. How could I say no? He led me in an encounter with the Father where He said the words, "Whether you take the medication or not, I will be with you." His words comforted me and strengthened my faith.

I decided to not take the meds one more night. The next day, no pain! And the next day, no pain! The third day of no pain, I knew I was healed! Three months later, we got pregnant with our first miracle baby. God did it with no help from doctors. Today, we have two beautiful, healthy children and are expecting our third. "O LORD, you have brought up my soul from Sheol; you restored me to life from among those who go down to the pit." Psalm 30:2. Glory be to the One who has the miracle working power!

~Brit Coppa

# Week 30

"Fear God and keep His commandments, for this is the duty of all mankind." ~*Ecclesiastes 12:13*

## READING PLAN

| | |
|---|---|
| Day 1: | Ecclesiastes 9-12 |
| Day 2: | Song of Solomon 1-4 |
| Day 3: | Song of Solomon 5-8 |
| Day 4: | Isaiah 1-5 |
| Day 5: | Isaiah 6-9 |
| Day 6: | Isaiah 10-13 |
| Day 7: | Rest Day/Catch Up |

## Faith in Action

Write a letter to God and thank Him for the opportunity to be reading His Word. Many people have lived their whole lives without having that opportunity.

Week 30    Date: _____

# *Journal Questions*

1. In Ecclesiastes 11:4 laziness and lack of effort does not give us the fruit or results we desire. Are you not seeing results or fruit because you're not doing the things that need to be done? How can you shift into being active to start reaping the fruit you want in your life?

2. Our relationship with God is seen as a marriage covenant. What do you think are a few keys to a good, loving marriage? What did you learn about our relationship with God through the illustration of marriage in the Song of Solomon?

3. How does Isaiah 5:20 apply to today? How can we keep ourselves protected from this deception?

4. Jesus and our Salvation was the plan from the beginning. What prophecies of Jesus do we see in the first few chapters of Isaiah? (Look at chapters 4, 7, 9, 11.)

# Week 30
## Reflection & Notes

## Gratitude

# Inspiration

I have always been very active; enjoying running, roller skating, skiing, and weight lifting. I had just had my fifth child, a cute, cuddly little girl. I had four sons from my first marriage, so I was used to being a boys' mom. Having my first girl was so exciting. Right after Katie turned nine months, I began running again. Right around that same time, I started experiencing a horrible pain under my arm when she would nurse. I didn't think anything of it until the night after I ran my first mile, in almost a year. When I finished, I noticed I had this numbness in my side and around my stomach. The next morning, my left eye and the side of my mouth started twitching. Within a few days, the numbness had spread throughout my body.

Off to the clinic I went since I didn't have a doctor at the time. Thankfully, I was seen by an amazing female doctor. I told her my story and past history. She took my bloodwork. She called me in two days and said she got me an appointment with a Neurologist. At the time, that was a miracle. They were booked out and they just happened to have had a cancellation that Monday. At that appointment, he tested me and had me get an MRI the next day. He had me come in on Friday and told me that it was Multiple Sclerosis and I needed to get into the hospital immediately. As I was leaving to go home and pack, I had my friend take me to the store to buy a jogging suit, determined to not wear a hospital gown.

My hospital stay was like a party. I had so many friends and family come to visit, and so many flowers and phone calls. The down side was being hooked up to IVs for 10 days, 8 hours a day. I began to pray and declare, "Jesus is healing my body." Listening to the Bible on tape at night when I would go to sleep brought me peace and rest. His Word is the healing power of Jesus. Watching aerobics programs and sporting events was also a daily highlight. I felt God remind me of Proverbs 29:18, *"Without a vision my people perish"* and Proverbs 23:7, *"As a man thinks in his heart so is he."*

After I was released from the hospital, I went to a Naturopath and began a diet of very clean and healthy food. I realized the numbness was going away as I focused on the healing power of Jesus. He kept showing me how much He loved me. By that summer, I was water skiing again and in the winter I was skiing and back running and weightlifting. During this time, I was advised by my doctor to not have any more children as it could be hard on my body. God had other plans, and two years later, I had my sweet daughter, Angie. I worked out five days a week while pregnant with her, up until three days before she was born.

Twenty-two years later, I got a pinched nerve and went back to my original Neurologist. After some testing, he said, "If you came to me and said you had MS, I would not believe you even though I am the doctor who diagnosed you. You have no signs of it at all." Praise God for His healing power!

~Maureen Brundage

*"For to us a child is born, to us a son is given; and the government shall be upon his shoulder, and his name shall be called Wonderful Counselor, Mighty God, Everlasting Father, Prince of Peace."* ~Isaiah 9:6

# Week 31

*"O Lord, You are my God. I will exalt You; I will praise Your name, for You have done wonderful things, plans formed of old, faithful and sure." ~Isaiah 25:1*

## READING PLAN

| | |
|---|---|
| Day 1: | Isaiah 14-17 |
| Day 2: | Isaiah 18-22 |
| Day 3: | Isaiah 23-27 |
| Day 4: | Isaiah 28-30 |
| Day 5: | Isaiah 31-35 |
| Day 6: | Isaiah 36-39 |
| Day 7: | Rest Day/Catch Up |

## Faith in Action

Encourage three people this week through an act of service, gift, a sweet note, or message.

Week 31    Date: _____

# Journal Questions

1. Part of the prophecy of Isaiah was a warning to people of certain lands to heed the voice of the Lord. Has there been a time when God has warned you to heed His voice? Did you hear and obey? What became of the situation?

2. Isaiah 24-28 teach us about trusting in the Lord and having hope in His promises. What primises are you trusting in the Lord?

3. What are some things we learn about God and His character in these chapters of Isaiah? What are things He is not pleased with?

4. Isaiah 29 prophecies of those that "draw near with their lips but their heart is far from Me." How do the two compare: drawing near with your lips versus drawing near with your heart?

# Week 31
## Reflection & Notes

## Gratitude

# Inspiration

I was a homeschool mom of nine children, pregnant with the tenth. There was a lot going on in my life, and one very difficult situation really consumed me. The storms raging around me started to impact me internally, creating a storm within. Nine babies in eighteen years and lots of sleepless nights had taken a toll on my mind and body.

When I was thinking hard about something, trying to figure it out on my own, I would start to feel like I was spinning and my eyes would roll back. I went to see a naturopathic doctor. She checked my pulse and immediately applied acupuncture. When she came back to the room after about twenty minutes, she said, "When you came in, you were on the verge of a Grand Mal Seizure." That seemed to explain why I wasn't feeling well.

I left the office that day trusting God with my next steps concerning the news I had received. This doctor closed her office shortly after that visit. It wasn't even an option to see her again and I did not plan to see another doctor about this illness. I felt led to work through this problem another way. As a daughter of God, I wanted to trust in the Spirit's leading and not lean of my own understanding this time. I brought the diagnosis to God and asked Him what He wanted to do about it.

When I would feel overwhelmed, the spinning would come on. My two older daughters would help with the other children so I could be alone in my room. Then I would lay down on my bed, where it was dark and quiet, and pray in the Spirit, in tongues to be specific. At that point in my life I didn't have the mind to come up with my own words to form a prayer, so praying in tongues was such a gift. This allowed me to pray with my prayer language from my spirit. God would strengthen me from that place. Totally relaxing my mind and casting all my cares on Him was crucial. I needed to roll all the anxieties and fears on Him so I could get well. I purposefully cleared my mind and allowed only the word of God to flow through my thoughts. I would declare, "No weapon formed against me shall prosper. By Your stripes I am healed." while laying in bed. By faith, I believed His words would come to pass.

My prayer time would take about a half an hour. Then I would get up and continue my normal routine with the family. This routine continued for about two weeks. By the end of the two weeks, the spinning had subsided enough so I didn't need to lay down anymore. Light spinning continued occasionally for another year or so. It was so minimal that it didn't interrupt my daily life at all. I just kept believing "I am healed, and this can't stay."

Finally, all spinning subsided, and I was completely healed! I praise God for His healing hand in my life. Hebrews 4:12 says, *"The Word of God is alive and active, and sharper than a double-edged sword."* Stand on His Word and apply it to your life. When you do, expect miracles!

~Jackie Dighans

"Trust in the Lord forever, for the Lord, the Lord himself, is the Rock eternal." ~Isaiah 26:4

# Week 32

"But those who wait on the Lord will renew their strength. They will soar on wings like eagles; they run and are not weary, they walk and do not faint." ~Isaiah 40:31

## READING PLAN

| | |
|---|---|
| Day 1: | Isaiah 40-43 |
| Day 2: | Isaiah 44-47 |
| Day 3: | Isaiah 48-51 |
| Day 4: | Isaiah 52-57 |
| Day 5: | Isaiah 58-62 |
| Day 6: | Isaiah 63-66 |
| Day 7: | Rest Day/Catch Up |

## Faith in Action

Share the story of salvation with someone or write out what He has done for you so you are ready to share with someone in the future.

Week 32     Date: _____

# Journal Questions

1. Isaiah 40 says that grass fades away and dies, flowers bloom and die, but the Word of God stands forever. How can this verse encourage you in whatever you are currently going through?

2. Isaiah 40:11 "He feeds His flock like a shepherd..." What is a shepherd, what is their role, and how do they care for their flock? How does a flock respond to their shepherd? What does it reveal to you about God?

3. God is over all, in all, and sees all. His ways are higher and greater than anything we can come up with on our own. Are you relying on His ways? How can you rely on His ways more than you have been?

4. Isaiah 53 is a prophecy about the Messiah and our salvation. What has the Messiah done for you in your life?

# Week 32
## Reflection & Notes

## Gratitude

# Inspiration

I woke up one morning to the Lord telling me how to dress for that day. I had already chosen my outfit but God commanded me to change into overalls and to top it off with a bandana. I assumed the bandana was for my hair but thought to myself it was an odd request. Nevertheless, I shoved the bandana in my pocket out of obedience.

I was on a mission trip in Colorado and our group had moved to a new service location at the last moment. We were to paint the home of an elderly couple. I was up on the ladder painting when I heard a horrifically loud crash. I was immediately transported off the ladder and I ran down the road knowing the Lord was leading me there.

At the scene of a terrifying wreck, I found a young girl around eight years old who had hit her head on the windshield so hard it broke and she was bleeding profusely. Grabbing the bandana from my pocket, I wrapped it around her head. It was still not enough to stop the tremendous amount of blood, so I wrapped my coveralls around her several times.

As I lifted the child out of the car, I could feel a crowd growing beside me. Looking left and right, I couldn't see anyone down the road. I knew there was an angelic presence beside me and I was absolutely certain they were assisting me. I was only fifteen and barely bigger than the child I was helping, yet I lifted the child out of the car effortlessly.

The child in my arms looked at me and then off to the side of me. I knew what she could see because I could feel the same presence as she asked, "What are you all doing here?"

Ironically, the little girl's name was Angel. The youth pastor took me to see her in the hospital later that day. When I walked into her room she pointed at me and said, "There's the angel! There's one of the angels!" I looked around the room for the angels I knew helped me out on the road as she met my eyes and said, "Where are the others?"

The pastor was stunned. He knew nobody else had been with me on that road. The experience shifted his perspective that day and opened his faith to the possibility of angels. We were told she should not have survived due to the type and severity of the head wound she suffered. The multitude of angels were there to guide me in saving her life. They had lifted me off the ladder and carried me down the road as time was compressed and actions occurred quickly. Even the fireman couldn't figure out how I got her out of the car based on the configuration of the windows and seat but it wasn't hard. I wasn't alone in pulling her out.

The Lord spoke to me in that encounter in a unique way. He will send us help, but sometimes He requires us to be His physical hands and feet. Angels were on the road that day guiding my every move. God will put us exactly where we need to be and He will send every resource required, even angelic beings for His purpose. He also requires obedience in the small things. If I hadn't changed, I wouldn't have had what was necessary to fulfill His purpose for me that day.

When you encounter really difficult things to endure and God gives you a tangible connection with the supernatural, your hope becomes solid and grounded in a reality greater than you. Ever since the crash, when I need my hope renewed, God sends me little white feathers that float down from midair to remind me that I am not alone.

*~Janice Gresser*

# Week 33

"Blessed is the man who trusts in the Lord, whose trust is the Lord." ~*Jeremiah 17:7*

## READING PLAN

| | |
|---|---|
| Day 1: | Jeremiah 1-4 |
| Day 2: | Jeremiah 5-8 |
| Day 3: | Jeremiah 9-11 |
| Day 4: | Jeremiah 12-15 |
| Day 5: | Jeremiah 16-20 |
| Day 6: | Jeremiah 21-23 |
| Day 7: | Rest Day/Catch Up |

## Faith in Action

Pray for people in your life that do not know or follow God. Pray for their eyes to be opened to His goodness and love.

Week 33   Date: _____

# *Journal Questions*

1. We have a choice in our walk with God, to follow His ways or our own. In what ways are you following Him? In what ways do you need to stop walking in your own ways and choose His instead?

2. We are told to tremble at His Word. What does this mean and how can you apply it to your life? (Isaiah 66:5, Jeremiah 5:22)

3. Jeremiah was sent to deliver an unpopular message to the people, but God promised to be with him. In what ways have you lost things or felt pressured because of following God? He promises to be with you.

4. Jeremiah 7 speaks of "trusting in false words from people speaking falsely." This still happens today. Falsehood doesn't profit. How can we recognize it? How can you protect against it?

# Week 33
## Reflection & Notes

## Gratitude

# Inspiration

It was a warm September day as I body surfed on the beach in California. I rode nearly a dozen waves before turning to find the best "wave of the day." I swam out quickly, noting excitedly that this one was far bigger than any of the preceding waves.

Pulling into the wave, I tucked my arms straight as an arrow expecting my head to emerge as the wave drew me toward the shore, but instead it continued to build, pulling water in front of it and exposing the sandy bottom. It quickly picked me up and thrust me head first into the hard packed ground. A shock wave whipped through me; I was instantly completely paralyzed. I knew at that moment I would be a quadriplegic for the rest of my life.

As my helpless body rolled beneath the thrashing wave. I tried lifting my head to take a gulp of air, but I could not move. I eventually blacked out, until I heard a voice directing others. I was on dry sand where lifeguards strapped me between two boards.

I was raced by ambulance to the nearest Trauma Center, and quickly hooked up to various machines. A few hours later, the hospital staff was surprised when the sensations in my body began to return gradually.

I welcomed the intense pain, it meant I was improving. I suddenly started to be able to move my body again! When the next medical attendant walked into my room, I announced my decision to go home. Several medical staff warned me that I should stay and that I could die on my way home. I replied, "I would rather die at home than here."

I was brought into the hospital on a stretcher, and countless people stared in disbelief when I walked out of the doors on my own.

Two weeks later, on my visit to see an orthopedic surgeon, he declared that I should have "died instantly on the beach that day." He told me in his "30-plus years of being in the medical field he had never seen X-rays like mine and could not explain how I was still alive!" When he explained what he saw in my X-rays, it was clear that God was looking out for me that day and that He was not through with me yet. My final prognosis was "extreme spinal shock." Miraculously, only the outer layers of my spinal cord were injured. Within eighteen months, it was as if I was never even injured.

Since my accident, friends and family ask if I was terrified in the ocean that day. Honestly, there was not one moment where I felt the slightest alarm, trauma or even worry. I remained unbothered even though I was certain I would be permanently paralyzed, and even when I thought I was going to drown.

That day I went bodysurfing alone, but when the wave crashed down upon me, I was no longer alone. A divine presence invited me to relax and remain peaceful. Instead of fear and panic, I felt curiosity and wonder. I enjoyed floating face down in the ocean without any control of my body. It was fascinating to be propelled along by the waves, feeling only my head like a football bobbing up and down in the ocean. I exclaimed to myself, "So this is what it is like to be paralyzed," while I imagined a new, life changing adventure. Instead of perceiving this event as a tragedy, I felt peace and comfort spoken to my heart.

The divine voice of God speaks peace and comfort to all of us, but it is up to us to receive the gift. No matter how heavy and dark your predicaments may seem, His presence will always be with you, to guide you past any frustration or discouragement

~Timothy Curtis

# Week 34

"For I know the plans I have for you, declares the Lord, plans for welfare and not for evil, to give you a future and a hope."
~Jeremiah 29:11

## READING PLAN

| | |
|---|---|
| Day 1: | Jeremiah 24-26 |
| Day 2: | Jeremiah 27-30 |
| Day 3: | Jeremiah 31-32 |
| Day 4: | Jeremiah 33-36 |
| Day 5: | Jeremiah 37-40 |
| Day 6: | Jeremiah 41-45 |
| Day 7: | Rest Day/Catch Up |

## Faith in Action

How can you help the poor, orphan and widow more than you are now? Make a plan on how you can help and act on it.

Week 34    Date: _____

# Journal Questions

1. Jeremiah was warning the people of what was to come, but God told them if they turned back He would remember their sin no more. Throughout the Bible God makes these types of if-then statements. Have you ever had God speak to you in this type of way? Describe.

2. God calls us to care for the poor, widow, and orphan and to not be greedy with gain. No matter your situation, how can you support the poor, widow and orphan?

3. Jeremiah 31 is the prophecy of the new covenant. This is the covenant we are in now that our Savior has come and died for us. Read and meditate on this chapter. Describe the new covenant.

4. It seems there's a pattern of God's people seeing Him work miracles, saving them, and then they forget and fall away. Why is it so easy for us to forget what He has done for us? Do you easily forget? How can you remember?

# Week 34
# Reflection & Notes

# Gratitude

# Inspiration

For 16 years, I reacted to eating gluten. In third grade, I went to the nurses office with a headache almost everyday. My mother picked me up from school early for weeks before we finally figured out that the culprit was gluten. We immediately cut it out of my diet almost completely. This was just the beginning of gluten taking things from me.

As I got older, the symptoms steadily grew worse. What began as a simple headache and an inability to sit through math class, turned into migraines that forced me to go home and lay in bed in a dark room. I threw up at a friend's birthday dinner because the restaurant cross-contaminated my meal and I didn't realize I had eaten gluten. My symptoms eventually evolved into flu-like body aches that lasted an entire week after I'd been "glutened."

Eventually, I went completely gluten free, but that still didn't solve my health problems and it caused me to miss out on so many experiences. I felt guilt and shame every time I went over to friends' houses and carefully investigated every meal or snack they made for me, in order to make sure I wouldn't get sick. Although I had a lot of options for gluten free meals, a strict gluten-free lifestyle took the joy and excitement away from meeting up with friends, attending birthday parties, and traveling. I lived with fear in the back of my mind that something I ate would put me in physical pain and cause me to miss out on all the fun. I don't believe we were created to only enjoy life halfway.

A year ago, a friend shared on Instagram that she was miraculously healed of Celiac Disease and Hashimoto's. As I read her post, I thought, "God, why is that possible for her and not for me?" He responded with an answer I didn't expect. "Why is it not possible for you?" I was not ready to go there, but every couple of months I thought about her story. If she could be healed then maybe it was possible for me. I don't remember what exactly changed for me, but in November I decided that I was tired of being gluten-free. I saw some of my friends eating a cinnamon roll, my favorite Saturday morning breakfast as a child, and got frustrated with the fact that I couldn't eat them. I wanted my own healing.

In December, I attended a conference at my church and I knew that healing was for me and it was happening that day. During prayer time, I ran up to a lady and asked her, "Will you pray with me that my celiac is gone and the fear doesn't hold me back any longer?" We prayed and I got exactly what I asked. I was able to take communion with the rest of the church for the first time in seven years. Since then, I can eat as much gluten as I want. I wasn't able to eat bread for most of my life. Now, I have so much joy, excitement, and gratitude. I no longer feel stress or fear when I travel. I get to celebrate birthdays without adjusting what I eat. I had read about all the miraculous stories of healings throughout the Bible, but for some reason I had forgotten that He is still doing healing miracles today!

~Mary DeAcetis

"At that time, declares the Lord, I will be the God of all the clans of Israel, and they shall be my people." ~Jeremiah 31:1

# Week 35

"It is He who made the earth by His power, who established the world by His wisdom, and by His understanding stretched out the heavens." ~*Jeremiah 51:15*

## READING PLAN

| | |
|---|---|
| Day 1: | Jeremiah 46-48 |
| Day 2: | Jeremiah 49-50 |
| Day 3: | Jeremiah 51-52 |
| Day 4: | Lamentations 1-2 |
| Day 5: | Lamentations 3-5 |
| Day 6: | Ezekiel 1-5 |
| Day 7: | Rest Day/Catch Up |

## Faith in Action

Pray and ask God to show you where you are trying to return to bondage or what bondage needs to be broken off.

Week 35     Date: _____

## Journal Questions

1. Jeremiah was beaten, put in prison, and eventually killed for speaking the words of God and begging people to repent. He was in a dark place. He could have given up on God, but he didn't. How have you handled the dark times in your life? Did you turn away from God?

2. A few people wanted Jeremiah to seek God for them and tell them what to do. Jeremiah came back with a message and warned them not to go back to Egypt. Egypt represented bondage. He warned them not to go back to bondage. What bondage has God delivered you from and what can you do to make sure you never turn back to it?

3. In Jeremiah 51:45, God tells Israel to come out of Babylon. Babylon represents the world and its lusts. How have you come out of Babylon? Are there ways or areas you still need to "come out of Babylon?"

4. The beginning of Ezekiel shares a vision he had of God and how He is holy. What does "holy" mean in Hebrew? Do you treat and perceive your relationship with God in the holiness He deserves?

# Week 35
# Reflection & Notes

# Gratitude

# INSPIRATION

That Sunday I rode my electric scooter into the sanctuary and worshiped with my family as I always did. Diagnosed with Primary Progressive MS two and a half years earlier, I no longer had feeling from my waist down.

Preaching on faith, my pastor closed the service telling congregants, "You really need to come to service tonight because I believe God is going to do something great."

On the drive home I looked at Pam and asked, "Do you think the reason God has not healed me is because I don't have enough faith?" "I don't know why God hasn't healed you, but I still believe He will." she replied. I nonchalantly stated, "I think we should attend service tonight." She agreed.

Attending Sunday services left me physically unable to leave my bed for days and that afternoon the tremors worsened significantly and my arms shook violently. I could barely speak but I told my wife, "I am not using my scooter. I'm going to walk in with my cane." That was almost a physical impossibility as a cane meant shuffling five feet on the best of days, but I did it.

The pastor stopped worship and declared, "I believe tonight God wants to restore what Satan has stolen from you." I knew that was spoken specifically for me. I wrote in large letters inside my bible, "HEALED OF MS, NOVEMBER 10, 1996" and soaked in the joy of that private moment, in the presence of the Holy Spirit, as the congregation continued their worship around me. I knew I was already healed. Holy Spirit instructed me to go forward for prayer. I questioned Him. "You have already healed me!" I got up and dutifully walked thirty feet to the altar forgetting my cane. I did not even comprehend what had happened. As I prayed on my knees, Holy Spirit instructed me to stand up, eyes closed, raise my hands and praise Him. I knew that was impossible with MS. That posture is one of the medical tests used in evaluation. As I stood praising God, eyes shut and arms up, it occurred to me that I had not fallen. My toes began tingling. I praised Him realizing I felt everything from the waist down. "Now go up the stairs."

There are 29 stairs to the balcony. In my excitement I decided to run three steps at a time and the Holy Spirit told me to do it without holding the railing. At the top, people cheered wildly. I ran back down the steps and up again a second time. There was an incredible sense of awe and His power and presence in my life at the top of those stairs. I was in the throne room of God.

When I finally saw Dr. Shapiro and he examined me, he sat down, drew a line on a sheet of paper, and said, "Wow. There is definitely power.....Tell me how this happened again?" I repeated my story and he whispered, "There's power." He asked about my medication. I joyfully confessed to flushing all 17 prescriptions down the toilet. He was shocked. "You can't do that, it will kill you! The last time we talked about you getting a job just to get out of the house a couple hours a week. Are you working part time?" I answered casually, "I went back to selling cars, working 60 hours a week and I'm going back to Bible college in a couple of months."

My doctor walked me up and down the hall like a circus act. "I can't explain this." He was astounded. "There is power. There is definitely power."

I had two more children because God healed everything. I finished Bible school and now serve as lead pastor. There is power!

~Robert Henklemann

# Week 36

"And I will give them one heart, and a new spirit I will put within them. I will remove the heart of stone from their flesh and give them a heart of flesh." ~*Ezekiel 11:19*

## READING PLAN

| | |
|---|---|
| Day 1: | Ezekiel 6-8 |
| Day 2: | Ezekiel 9-13 |
| Day 3: | Ezekiel 14-16 |
| Day 4: | Ezekiel 17-19 |
| Day 5: | Ezekiel 20-22 |
| Day 6: | Ezekiel 23-25 |
| Day 7: | Rest Day/Catch Up |

## Faith in Action

Pray daily for discernment, "God, please give me eyes to see Your truth and ears to hear Your words. God, please allow me to have a discerning spirit and recognize Your truth above all else. Amen."

Week 36    Date: _____

## *Journal Questions*

1. Ezekiel prophesied to the leaders that they were leading the people astray. We are all leaders in some way. How can we heed this warning as leaders? In what ways can we unknowingly lead someone astray?

2. What are qualities of a good leader? How can you develop those qualities in your own life?

3. In Ezekiel 16, God reminds the people of all that He had done for them. He made them His lovely bride, but the Israelites went astray following their own lusts and trusting in themselves. When things are going well and right, do you tend to stay near to God and give Him the glory, or do you turn to yourself and put God "back up on the shelf?"

4. God warns about false prophets all throughout Scripture. According to Ezekial, who does God consider a false prophet? (Ezekiel 13)

## Week 36
## Reflection & Notes

## Gratitude

# Inspiration

When I left my nursing career to be home and raise my seven amazing children, I discovered I didn't know who I was aside from my roles as a wife and mother. My life was defined by deep seated fears, trauma and loss. Moreover, I struggled with my health and knew that if I didn't enact radical changes in my life, I could die.

When this woman, Summer Dey, approached me about a coaching program, I came up with every excuse not to do it, but God crushed every one of them. My biggest emotional hurdle was money, yet God reminded me that I was worth the investment and He would satisfy my needs.

At the same time I began coaching, I also started to struggle with colitis, a new illness now added to my growing list of intestinal disorders. I grew sicker each day until I was eventually hospitalized. During the forty-five days in the hospital, I committed to showing up for every online coaching session. Although I never left the house without makeup, I was determined to show up on that zoom call just as I was: hospital gown, tubes and all.

My condition worsened. After I was diagnosed with a rare type of diverticulitis and perforated bowel, and was transferred to another facility. In spite of my worsening condition, I remained dedicated to coaching and refused to give up on the opportunity God provided. I minimized my dose of pain medicine in order I could fully participate.

When I signed up for coaching, I didn't realize I would be with a group of women. I had a huge issue trusting women. I believed the lie that I didn't need friends in my life. God knew better.

As I lay on my sick bed, life draining from my body, Summer asked a member of our group, Jessica, to share a prophetic message she had received. She shared, "I prayed for health and life and then I felt a ball of euphoria move from my heart into my throat and out my mouth and I spoke in tongues. I saw Shannon in a war zone, on her hands and knees, face to the ground. My vision was in tones of black and gray, everything consumed by shadows, including Shannon, until we, her group of sisters, came to her engulfed in light. Summer was out in front taking charge. Shannon remained in her position, hopeless and helpless, but we stood guard over her like elephants protecting their young from lions. Strength grew in that circle of light. We kept watch, protecting her until she was able to get up again."

The next morning I had surgery to remove a foot of my colon. My health deteriorated and I could barely utter a prayer. My family couldn't visit because of Covid and I believed I was losing my battle with death, but these women continued to pray and put the full armor of God on me daily. They battled alongside me, picked me up out of the ashes, and kept me spiritually protected. I had shield maidens with me on this battlefield. All glory to God!

The battle was won and I was released from the hospital. I had suffered with colon pain since I was four years old. I got healed completely from a lifetime of physical pain and in over two years it has never come back. God not only healed my health through that experience, but He healed my soul as well. I no longer believe the lie of the enemy that I don't need women in my life. Through it all, God has shown me who I am. He has surrounded me with warrior women who are now my nearest and dearest friends. I truly believe I would not have survived without their constant prayers.

~*Shannon Gort Eckhoff*

# Week 37

"I will sprinkle clean water on you, and you shall be clean from all your uncleannesses, and from all your idols I will cleanse you."
~Ezekiel 36:25

## READING PLAN

| | |
|---|---|
| Day 1: | Ezekiel 26-28 |
| Day 2: | Ezekiel 29-32 |
| Day 3: | Ezekiel 33-36 |
| Day 4: | Ezekiel 37-39 |
| Day 5: | Ezekiel 40-41 |
| Day 6: | Ezekiel 42-45 |
| Day 7: | Rest Day/Catch Up |

## Faith in Action

Study about the Sabbath and pray and ask God what it means for you in your walk with Him.

Week 37     Date: _____

## *Journal Questions*

1. God talks about the Sabbath often as "My Sabbath(s)" and as a "sign between Me and you" (Ezekiel 20:20). Why do you think He would call it His? (Verses to reference: Genesis 1:3, Exodus 16:26, 20:8, 31:15-16, Leviticus 19:3,13, 26:2, Deuteronomy 5:12, Isaiah 58:13, 66:23, Ezekiel 22:8, Matthew 12:8-12, 24:20, Mark 2:27, Acts 15:21, Hebrews 4:9.)

2. Do you keep a Sabbath? Why or why not? What would it look and feel like if you did?

3. Nothing unclean is to be in or around His temple (Ezekiel 44). His Spirit lives in us. What unclean thing is "in your temple" that He may be asking you to let go of? Is there anything you are secretly hiding? He's waiting for you to release it so you can be clean and pure before Him.

4. Ezekiel was given a message by God and was told to deliver it even though they wouldn't listen. Who are you assigned to in your life to give a message from God? (Children, co-workers, family, friends, clients?) Are you sharing it even if they aren't always receptive?

# Week 37
# Reflection & Notes

# Gratitude

# INSPIRATION

My wife and I took a leap of faith. I stepped down from my position as a youth pastor in one of the largest churches in the nation to plant a new church, thinking everyone would support me. That didn't happen, and as a consequence, we lost everything. Homeless with two young children, one of our first church members invited us to live in his half finished garage. I often fed my family of four at Wendy's by taking advantage of the 4 for $4 deal.

During that time, I accepted an invitation to speak on a cruise. A controversial pastor took his place at the podium and shortly into his message half the audience walked out. I began to follow them, but I heard God command, "Sit down!" The evening's talk was entitled "Let It Be." The pastor assured us that if we were to sow a seed and write our prayers on the back of the offering envelope, they would be answered before we got home.

I boldly scribbled "HEALTH" and asked my wife, "How much?" "You already know," she said. "Oh dear God, please don't say that," I responded quickly. "You know," she nodded. We had $870. To address my health issues I needed a $30,000 surgery. I looked at a friend, "Do you have gas money to get us home? If I give this I will have nothing left." I took the risk and trusted God with my money. When the talk was over and my money was gone, I used a permanent marker on my forearm and wrote "Let It Be."

All the big names made fun of the preacher, accusing him of stealing people's money. They declared people idiots for giving away their rent money. I adjusted my sleeve to hide the Sharpie tattoo. God rebuked me, "If you don't show them, I will take the blessing." I held up my arm. "It's me. I am one of those stupid people." They taunted and jeered, "We will see how your electricity bill turns out!"

As we exited I noticed an older couple in the VIP room. They kept to themselves the entire night and no one welcomed them. I told them I appreciated them being on the cruise and invited them to hear me speak.

The next day, we disembarked for our journey home to Georgia. Half way home, I opened my email. "I heard you talking about your health concerns. My sister is a doctor and I would like to share with you a surgery that could help..." I braced for the lecture about what I should be doing to take care of myself and read the next line in total shock. "By the time you get home, there should be a check in your mailbox for $30,000. I don't care what you do with the money because I loved your testimony, but you need to have this procedure."

We arrived home to find a check for $30,000. Stunned and incredibly grateful, I called the phone number listed on the email. A gentleman answered and I immediately recognized his voice as the older gentleman from the cruise. He could not have known I had given away all of my money. I thanked him for believing in me but he quickly corrected me, "I don't believe in you. I don't just give out money. God told me to do this. I don't care what you do with the money but God told me it is specifically for the procedure."

My investment of $870 was everything I had, but it was small compared to what God did. My trust in God to fulfill His promises and meet my needs blessed me greater than I could've imagined. To this day, there is a tattoo on my forearm that reads, "Let It Be" ... and I have.

*~Chris Dorrity*

# Week 38

"How great are His signs, how mighty His wonders! His kingdom is an everlasting kingdom, and His dominion endures from generation to generation." ~*Daniel 4:3*

## READING PLAN

| | |
|---|---|
| Day 1: | Ezekiel 46-48 |
| Day 2: | Daniel 1-3 |
| Day 3: | Daniel 4-6 |
| Day 4: | Daniel 7-9 |
| Day 5: | Daniel 10-12 |
| Day 6: | Hosea 1-4 |
| Day 7: | Rest Day/Catch Up |

## Faith in Action

Step outside of yourself this week and do an act of service to help someone in need.

Week 38   Date: _____

# Journal Questions

1. In Daniel chapter 1, the king gives Daniel a new name. Why? Are there any names that you have taken on that are not the names God has called you?.

2. In Daniel 3, the three Hebrew men were hard pressed to violate God's command and bow down to an idol and worship it. They stood strong in their faith and were willing to die to obey God's word. Re-read and reflect on their responses to the king. What does it show you?

3. In Daniel 6, the Enemy goes after Daniel's prayer life. It would have been easy for Daniel to make excuses or adjustments or simply wait out the time. He does not. He understands the source of His strength is his time with God. Are you tenacious in protecting your prayer time?

4. In Daniel 10, we find principalities and powers of darkness ruling regions and opposing the work of God. Reflect on what the powers of darkness may be opposing in your life. Pray that God would bring breakthroughs in these areas.

# Week 38
## Reflection & Notes

## Gratitude

# INSPIRATION

On September 20, 2020, while I was sitting in my car, I was hit by a truck. At the time, I had barely just recovered from a spinal rupture which paralyzed me. Ten years into that healing process I went from not being able to walk, to hiking in Sedona, to sitting in my car and being run over by a truck.

I got out of the car wondering how that happened? I turned to the driver and asked if he was on his phone. He lied and said I pulled out in front of him. I was parked at the end of a driveway in a residential neighborhood but he lied to the officers. I tried to make sense of it until someone came over and informed us they had a video and that I had been at a complete standstill. The video showed he was not paying attention.

I had major spinal cord injuries but I refused surgery to try the natural route. After two years of suffering, another MRI showed the nerve between the C6 and C7 discs was still impinged and I was tired of the continuous pain. I was anxious to be at my highest potential so I consented to surgery. Two weeks later I went to my office to turn on the light and was hit with a posterior stroke. My subdural artery had been dissected during surgery.

The likelihood of living through a posterior stroke is only 15%. I not only survived, but I thrived, staying committed to everything I had committed to previously: I did a brand photo shoot, I flew to Mexico with my team six weeks later, and I got on a stage and spoke!

When I got hit by the truck I realized I wasn't following the right path. I had left nursing for a bit but didn't trust myself to build my own business, nor did I have enough faith in God to follow His plan. I realized that if I didn't listen and didn't let go of what was not serving me to pursue my bigger purpose, then I was going to be shifted.

Getting hit by that truck got me off of the path I was on and set me on a new one. I lost all of my income. Ironically I had previously abandoned my business to go back to nursing for the safety and security of that income, but the very thing that I thought I was supposed to do was taken away. That next year I built my own business, my income went up 400%, and I became a top leader in 25 countries.

As I progressed through my healing journey there were many lessons, blessings, and beautiful occurrences that taught me to have faith and to stay in the present. My faith and belief grew as my relationship with God grew deeper and stronger. He continuously put people in my life that helped me develop a connection to Him.

I saw all of the events as a blessing and handed complete control over to the Lord. The situation was a test to live out my faith. Because of that test, I developed a deeper wisdom and clarity about life.

The chance of developing another clot was very high in the first weeks and months. I had to learn to walk out my faith even with the reality that there was no safety in my own body except to know that God had me.

Are you going to walk your talk and stay with it even in the bad times? Do you really believe? Will you truly surrender? I learned to trust, surrender, and give up control to God. Because I am so confident and grounded in the message of faith now, I can share it with absolute conviction. My test has become my testimony.

~Jenell Kelly

# Week 39

"But I am the Lord your God from the land of Egypt; you know no God but me, and besides me there is no savior." ~*Hosea 13:4*

## READING PLAN

| | |
|---|---|
| Day 1: | Hosea 5-9 |
| Day 2: | Hosea 10-14 |
| Day 3: | Joel 1-3 |
| Day 4: | Amos 1-5 |
| Day 5: | Amos 6-9 |
| Day 6: | Obadiah 1, Jonah 1-4 |
| Day 7: | Rest Day/Catch Up |

## Faith in Action

Ask someone in your life that you haven't always been patient with for forgiveness. You can try saying, "Please forgive me for not always being patient with you when I could have been."

Week 39  Date: _____

## Journal Questions

1. The book of Hosea is a prophecy about the adultery of Israel. God likens our relationship with Him to a husband and wife. When Israel was walking out of line with God's ways, He told them they were in adultery. What picture does that give you for God's desire for us as His bride? How would you expect a faithful bride/wife to act, behave, think and treat you?

2. Are you acting like a faithful bride toward God? How can you improve in the ways that you show up in your relationship with God?

3. Jonah tried to run away from what God was calling him to do. God made his path of travel difficult until Jonah repented and turned back to God and submitted to His will. Has there ever been a time in your life where you ran from what God was calling you to do? How did that turn out?

4. Are there times when God has given you a warning? Did you heed the warning? Why or why not? How can you improve in this area?

# Week 39
## Reflection & Notes

## Gratitude

# INSPIRATION

My husband and I struggled to put our lives back together after a short lived relapse with meth. We were saved but not following the Lord, going to church here and there, but not walking closely. I discovered I was pregnant and everything changed. Cody and I surrendered to the Lord and got married. It was in this new life that the enemy tried to shake us, but "what he intended for evil, God turned to good to accomplish what is now being done and the saving of many lives."

At ten weeks, doctors diagnosed my unborn child with Trisomy 18, defined as "incompatible with life." Less than 6% born with this congenital disorder make it to two weeks, most are miscarried or die in the womb. Hospitals and staff refuse life saving treatment for affected infants and people must fly to other countries to get care. Medical staff urged me to abort Trinity and chastised me for refusing. I had 14 abortions in my past and repeated broken promises to God to never do it again. Satan used my past against me: "You've aborted 14 babies, this time is okay." It seemed easy to justify this one but I refused.

God however, had words of life for us. Cody and I attended a meeting visited by a prophet from Georgia. "That baby you are carrying inside you will live and not die. You will have everything you need. Do not worry." Those were the first words of hope we could hang on to. We declared them from that moment on. Even as Doctors spoke death over Trinity into my late pregnancy, God comforted us with His words, "I said what I said, I know what it looks like but trust my word not what you are seeing."

Trinity was stillborn. They laid her dead body on me and told me to take a few last minutes with her. I refused and asked them to treat her like any other infant and do everything to rescue her. The begrudgingly laid her limp body on a table and she began to breathe. They gasped in shock as the Lord revived her. Trinity was taken to NICU and given to one nurse to hook her up to equipment and keep her stable. There are usually three or four nurses but Trinity's nurse was alone and later confessed she was shocked to be left alone, "that baby was so complex but something came over me to guide my hands -it must have been 'God!'" She said when they wheeled her in the room something changed. There was peace. When God says it's a Go it's a Go - one nurse or ten.

Every single doctor who refused to treat our child conceded one by one and even laid hands on her body as we prayed over her before medical interventions. One doctor testified that he felt peace to take certain enormous risks in surgery knowing it was okay because God guided his hands. The only unrelenting doctor was a cardiac surgeon. He would not treat Trinity's failing heart and gave her two weeks. However, a scan done before they released us found a stenosis which appeared out of nowhere tightened her valve and balanced her heart, buying her enough time to grow big enough for open heart surgery at age four.

Trinity is five now and her testimony has saved other babies and cemented our marriage in spite of Satan's statistics, and our family is thriving! God is the supernatural glue that holds us together. Even in our worst times, He removes that extra burden. He is eternal no matter what he decides for Trinity's life. Every day he grants us is an extra blessing and if He takes her, she will be home with Him.

*~Nina Williams*

# Week 40

"He has told you, O man, what is good; and what does the Lord require of you but to do justice, and to love kindness, and to walk humbly with your God?" ~*Micah 6:8*

## READING PLAN

| | |
|---|---|
| Day 1: | Micah 1-4 |
| Day 2: | Micah 5-7 |
| Day 3: | Nahum 1-3, Habakkuk 1-3 |
| Day 4: | Zephaniah 1-3 |
| Day 5: | Haggai 1-2 |
| Day 6: | Zechariah 1-7 |
| Day 7: | Rest Day/Catch Up |

## Faith in Action

God created us to be a blessing. Find a way that you can be a blessing to someone this week.

Week 40    Date: _____

# Journal Questions

1. God is very patient with His people. He warns them numerous times and encourages them to come back to Him and His ways. He is a patient, loving Father. In what ways could you do a better job of being patient with the people in your life?

2. The prophets are the ones that heard from God often and would receive messages from Him to share. Sometimes, they wouldn't hear from Him for weeks, months, or years at a time. Have you experienced a time of "silence" from hearing God? How did you handle it?

3. When you feel as if you are not hearing from God, do you stop talking or asking Him things, or do you continue to press forward until you hear from Him?

4. Have there been times when you have given up hope in God answering you? Repent, ask Him to forgive you, and turn back to Him and His ways. He is a faithful friend.

# Week 40
## Reflection & Notes

## Gratitude

# Inspiration

In 2005, I was finishing up my last semester of college when hurricane Katrina hit New Orleans. I evacuated to my hometown in Arkansas with only one change of clothes and my laptop. Watching the coverage of the devastation over the next few months pulled me into a deep depression. Less than a year after Katrina, I was diagnosed with multiple pain conditions and prescribed opiate painkillers, leading me into addiction and allowing me to escape a multitude of pain and trauma from my past.

A few years later friends and family staged an intervention, and I spent a month in an expensive drug rehabilitation program, but I wasn't ready for recovery. There was more to come before I would hit rock bottom.

After my first rehab, I found myself in an abusive relationship with a man who isolated me from my loved ones and furthered my addiction into IV drugs. In the back of my mind, I knew God was holding me up through the physical abuse and drug overdoses. Having the support from friends and family, I found the strength to leave the abuse and work toward rebuilding my life. But I still refused to get the help I really needed. For the next couple years, I battled my depression. I attempted to pursue my career path with highs and lows along the way.

February 13, 2010, was a significant blow. My grandfather, the most important person in my life, committed suicide after battling a long illness. Falling back into my addiction and depression, two years to the day after his death, I decided I couldn't fight anymore. I walked to the bathroom and downed a bottle of Tylenol, believing this was the answer to my suffering. But God had other plans.

Within hours, and through a series of miraculous events, most of which I don't remember (but was later told), an angel discovered me and called an ambulance. I was rushed to the ER, spent three days in the ICU, then admitted to the psych ward for evaluation. Upon meeting the psychiatric doctor and looking over my medical records, he recommended I spend a minimum of six months in a drug recovery program. I found his advice so ridiculous I literally laughed in his face, telling him, "No way, that's not going to happen." That evening the pain and hopelessness came back in full force. Whaling in pain, with no other options, I knelt onto the cold, tile floor of my hospital room, praying the only words I could find, "God, help me!" Muttering just those three words, I cried myself to sleep.

God heard my cry. The next morning, I woke with a feeling that can only be described as a *"peace that surpasses all understanding"* [Phil 4:7]. I had the willingness and determination I had lacked before in my recovery. Meeting with the doctor again, I told him I was ready for long-term treatment. A woman named Dorcas, the same angel who called the ambulance, was the director of a local women's recovery program. Calling her from the psych ward, I enrolled in the program.

A week into the program, God would send me a second angel. Sarah would become my spiritual mother. Meeting weekly, she re-introduced me to a God who loved me entirely, no matter what mistakes I'd made in my past. On March 12, 2012, one month after attempting to take my own life, I accepted Jesus into my heart. Meeting with Sarah weekly, I began reading through the Bible. After graduating from the program, I joined Sarah's Bible study group with 10 other sisters in Christ who walked with me for the first decade of my recovery. Through this walk I found my life scripture. *Galatians 5:1, "For Freedom Christ has set us free; therefore, stand firm, and do not submit again to a yoke of slavery."*

~Allison Johnson

# Week 41

"You are the light of the world. A city set on a hill cannot be hidden." ~*Matthew 5:14*

## READING PLAN

| | |
|---|---|
| Day 1: | Zechariah 8-14 |
| Day 2: | Malachi 1-4 |
| Day 3: | Matthew 1-4 |
| Day 4: | Matthew 5-7 |
| Day 5: | Matthew 8-10 |
| Day 6: | Matthew 11-13 |
| Day 7: | Rest Day/Catch Up |

## Faith in Action

Spend some time in prayer and walk through forgiving someone that has lied to you in the past that caused hurt, anger or bitterness. Forgive them, bless them, and release them. Do this just between you and God.

Week 41         Date: _____

# Journal Questions

1. Look up the meaning of each of the prophet's names that we read this week and write them out below. For example, "Zechariah" means "God has remembered." There is meaning in the names of people that God uses.

2. Chronologically, Malachi is the last book written before Jesus came, and then we were given the gospels. Could this book have significance in what's written? What is the message you've learned overall from what this prophet wrote?

3. When Jesus was tempted by the devil in the wilderness, He responded with scripture. What's your first reaction when temptation or accusation comes your way? How can you start using scripture in your defense?

4. In Matthew 8, Jesus heals ten lepers and only one returns to Him to thank Him and give Him praise. That's just 10 percent! Are you quick to give God praise when He answers your prayers, or blesses you in some way? Do you lean toward the 10 percent camp of thanksgiving or the 90 percent that never returned with praise?

# Week 41
## Reflection & Notes

## Gratitude

# Inspiration

As a young mother, pain and sickness entered my life through a disease called fibromyalgia. The doctors had no answers. My health steadily declined over the next fourteen years and my little family suffered with me. In a frantic quest for answers, I read over one hundred self-help books. Nevertheless, I continued deteriorating down to 82 pounds as I was only able to eat two food options for three years.

Life flooded out of my body. My core body temperature dropped to 83 degrees. Years of malnutrition, acute sensitivities and numerous allergies wrecked my body and I was crashing. Hospitals terrified me, but in my desperation, I agreed to go.

Triage nurses immediately checked me into critical care, hooked me up to IV therapy and put me on a hot bed. The hospital released me six days later, but complications and reactions to the IV therapy decimated my memory. It was another crushing blow. My husband and I were hopeless.

Two months after my hospital stay, my husband and I happened upon a television preacher we had never watched before. As I listened, my heart burned with hope as they shared, "God desires to do miracles for us because of His immeasurable love." I listened intently as he continued, "If you have lost a family member, if your business has failed, or if you are sick, Jesus wants to answer your prayers." In desperation, I finally cried out to God. I said the sinner's prayer and was born again. I surrendered every one of my weaknesses to God. He came in a powerful light and loved me and forgave me right where I was at.

Jesus directed me to seek prayer for healing. I lay on a sleeping bag in the back of our jeep, as my husband drove to prayer meetings each week. Miracles piled upon miracles as hundreds of believers prayed for me. They instructed me to forgive everyone, including myself, and then God would give me the authority to tell the sickness to leave my body. One year later, my faith grew strong enough to believe God could do anything and to take hold of His promises for healing. I was passionately in love with Jesus! From head to toe, Jesus healed me and saved me when no doctor could figure out my case.

Through the many trials, I learned valuable elements to living a full, rich life: asking this wildly loving Jesus into our hearts and believing He can restore. Jesus is the good news. He wants all of us to know His plan of salvation and to know the riches of His promises. Our hearts can be broken in so many different ways, but our God is in the business of restoration. He can bring you back to life and give you measurably more than what you lost. His big, loving arms can heal the worst of circumstances. If your heart is broken and you are not living the life you hoped for, pray and ask God for salvation. Give your life to Him and He will come into your heart. He is eager to help you. You are meant to run with the King!

*~Nancy Ann Johnson, Author of "Ask for Your Miracle"*

*"But seek first the kingdom of God and his righteousness, and all these things will be added to you." ~Matthew 6:33*

# Week 42

*"Go therefore and make disciples of all nations, baptizing them in the name of the Father and of the Son and of the Holy Spirit"*
*~Matthew 28:19*

## READING PLAN

| | |
|---|---|
| Day 1: | Matthew 14-16 |
| Day 2: | Matthew 17-19 |
| Day 3: | Matthew 20-22 |
| Day 4: | Matthew 23-25 |
| Day 5: | Matthew 26-28 |
| Day 6: | Mark 1-4 |
| Day 7: | Rest Day/Catch Up |

## Faith in Action

Add to the *Praise Report* in the back of this journal and give God some praise this week.

Week 42          Date: _____

# Journal Questions

1. Jesus tells us to ask whatever we desire according to His will and to believe that we will receive it. What does it mean to pray "according to His will?"

2. Are you asking boldly for things in your prayers? In what ways could you improve this?

3. In Matthew 15:6-9, Jesus calls a group of Pharisees "hypocrites" and rebukes them for holding their man-made traditions over the Word of God. God sees our heart and knows our intentions. Are there any areas in your life where you appear one way but your heart is far from Him?

4. Jesus often withdrew to pray. He knew the importance of finding a quiet place to be with His heavenly Father. Is withdrawing to pray a practice in your life? Reflect.

# Week 42
## Reflection & Notes

## Gratitude

# Inspiration

I have always believed I am a powerful woman of God. He has given me great influence in the lives of those around me. The Lord has filled me with His power to accomplish great things. Here's the story of the one time He used me to miraculously heal someone.

I attended a weekly single moms' fellowship group. We called our group "Overcomers" and met to bare one another's burdens and pray over each other. We bore our souls without shame as we cried, got angry, comforted, and encouraged each other. This was an environment free of judgment and condemnation. The Lord, through our sisters, ministered to us truth, comfort, strength, hope, joy, life, healing, courage, and faith!

One night, we arrived late and I came in quietly. A few minutes later, another one of our members came in late with a new lady none of us knew. As this new mama walked past me, the Holy Spirit spoke to my spirit and said, "Get up. Anoint her stomach and pray for healing."

I would love to tell you I immediately obeyed, but I did not. I sat there and debated with the God of all creation. Have you ever done that? Well, it doesn't work! The Holy Spirit burned inside of me for the duration of our fellowship time. The Lord had healing to impart and He wasn't going to let my momentary lack of faith stop that.

Fellowship ended and we began to pray. The new mama spoke up and asked for prayer to heal her terminal cancer in her stomach. I immediately told her what God had said to me the moment she entered the room and I asked permission to anoint her stomach and pray over her. She informed us all she did not believe in God, but she was out of options and the doctors gave her only weeks to live.

Another woman felt led by the Holy Spirit to anoint her head and pray, so I pulled frankincense oil from my purse and together we anointed her head and stomach. We prayed in faith for healing, salvation and peace of mind as we let the Holy Spirit minister through us.

The next week, this lady reported back to us that her cancer was completely gone and she had been healed! She declared she now believed in the God who healed her and she planned to go to church that week. Hallelujah!

Just two weeks later, this newly saved mama died in a tragic fire. I learned that day, through many tears, the eternal importance of obeying the Holy Spirit's leading, no matter what! A person's eternal salvation may be on the other side of your absolute obedience to minister to them.

You are a powerful person too! The power of the Holy Spirit dwells inside of you. You are capable of doing exceedingly, abundantly above all you can ask, think or imagine!

You have miracles inside of you waiting to be released in the name of Jesus, if you will have the faith to believe and the courage to act on that belief.

~Maya Baker

"When the Son of Man comes in his glory, and all the angels with him, then he will sit on his glorious throne." ~Matthew 25:31

# Week 43

"Watch and pray so that you will not fall into temptation. The spirit is willing, but the flesh is weak." ~*Mark 14:38*

## READING PLAN

| | |
|---|---|
| Day 1: | Mark 5-7 |
| Day 2: | Mark 8-10 |
| Day 3: | Mark 11-13 |
| Day 4: | Mark 14-16 |
| Day 5: | Luke 1-2 |
| Day 6: | Luke 3-5 |
| Day 7: | Rest Day/Catch Up |

## Faith in Action

Spend extra time in prayer this week. "Father, help me to see the areas I need to improve. Help my unbelief. Help me understand You and Your Word at a deeper level. Where am I falling short? Where do I need to increase my faith? You are good and worthy of all praise. Amen."

Week 43     Date: _____

## *Journal Questions*

1. What comes out of our mouths is a reflection of our heart. Jesus rebuked the men for caring more about what they ate than how they spoke and acted (Mark 7:21-23). Are there any areas of the different defilements listed in these verses where you need improvement?

2. Jesus corrects the disciples for looking for position and power rather than looking to serve. Are there areas in your life where you might be making the same mistake?

3. In Mark 11, Jesus describes His house as a house of prayer. Do you feel like prayer is a priority in the church? What are ways you might encourage more prayer in your local fellowship?

4. You are called to receive the reign of God as a little child. What does this mean? What does the faith of a child look like? In what ways could you walk with more child-like faith?

# Week 43
# Reflection & Notes

## Gratitude

# Inspiration

I was raised Jewish. In the 1990's, I moved from New York City to Hawaii for graduate school. While there, I learned about the Jewish Messiah, Jesus, and how He fulfilled all of the prophecies I learned about while growing up. I was so excited to share my faith with others and started to do so when a Japanese friend of mine invited me to meet at the local hospital to pray for the sick. I had never done this before.

We walked down the halls praying and we felt God lead us to a room with a sick father. He was hooked up to machines and was unconscious. His two daughters and wife were in the room crying. We circled his bed, held hands, and began to pray. As we were praying, I heard the still small voice of God prompt me to prophesy the man would be healed in three days. I told one daughter and she became angry. She said, "My father is about to die. How can you say such a thing?" The other daughter said she believed, and prayed with us for this to happen.

The next day, we returned and witnessed a miracle. He was able to move his shoulder and other parts of his body. The daughters and mother got on their knees and prayed fervently. Shortly after, they purchased Bibles. The following day I came in to pray for him again, and his eyes were open. He was still hooked up to a heart machine and kept trying to get the tubes out of his throat. The doctor said, "This is a miracle. He should not be alive. He had a ten percent chance of living." I told the doctor I am not surprised because I prayed to Jesus and He answered the prayer.

The third day, I did not return, but I received a phone call from my friend who said he had been moved to a different floor and was no longer in the ICU. I came back on the fourth day and met many more of his family members. They were all smiling from ear to ear, glowing. They all purchased Bibles. Their father reached out to take my hand. He was healed! We continued to go to the prayer chapel to pray with family members. We saw many more miracles.

Another miracle that really stuck out to me happened when we decided to walk down the hall and ask God where He wanted to take us. We felt led to enter a room. To my surprise, one of my clients, who I had been praying for, was in this room. His grandmother was dying. She was Japanese and a Buddhist. My friend, who was with me, had converted from Buddhism to Christianity and was able to explain to her the good news that Jesus takes away sins in Japanese. The next time I saw him he had told all my coworkers the testimony of his grandmother's salvation and healing.

God's miracles may be waiting on our "yes!"

~Rhonda Gordon

"And he said to them, 'Go into all the world and proclaim the gospel to the whole creation,'" ~Mark 16:15

# Week 44

"Strive to enter through the narrow door. For many, I tell you, will seek to enter and will not be able." ~*Luke 13:24*

## READING PLAN

| | |
|---|---|
| Day 1: | Luke 6-7 |
| Day 2: | Luke 8-9 |
| Day 3: | Luke 10-12 |
| Day 4: | Luke 13-15 |
| Day 5: | Luke 16-19 |
| Day 6: | Luke 20-22 |
| Day 7: | Rest Day/Catch Up |

## Faith in Action

Jesus commands His followers to be quick to forgive and to forgive "seventy times seven." What unforgiveness are you storing up in your heart against someone? Do you need to call them, text them or write them a letter releasing them from the bitterness you have against them? Or maybe just pray and forgive them. Unforgiveness keeps you trapped and a "prisoner." It's time to forgive.

Week 44   Date: _____

## *Journal Questions*

1. Jesus asked his followers to leave everything and follow Him. What do you think He meant by that? What might it mean for you to "leave everything" and follow Him?

2. Is there something you need to "leave" to follow Him? What is He asking you to surrender and leave behind?

3. When we put our belief and trust in the Son, our sin is forgiven. Are there places you need to forgive others with the same compassion that God has shown to you?

4. In Luke 12:22, Jesus said to His disciples, "Do not worry about your life." When we worry, we are not walking in faith. What worries do you have that you are ready to surrender to God so you can live in more faith?

# Week 44
## Reflection & Notes

## Gratitude

# Inspiration

*Do not neglect to show hospitality to strangers, for thereby some have entertained angels unawares.*

- Hebrews 13:2

I have had a run in with an angel on three separate occasions. They have all been full of chaos and panic as if the devil created distractions to keep me from positive encounters. All three times I didn't realize who I was entertaining until after it was over. In fact, I mistook my guardian angel for an enemy.

We had renovated a new house for six months and it was finally ready. In preparation for our move, I had scheduled cleaners and drove to the house to move in a few things.

As I passed through our rural neighborhood, I saw two young men walking up the hill. One of them was dressed from head to toe in black leather with silver studs all over his jacket and pants. He looked extremely out of place. People in that neighborhood didn't dress like that and the weather was hot. He looked like trouble.

Our move was postponed the following day because my husband, Tim, was in the hospital. Alone, I drove to the new house to let the cleaners in. Since I didn't know the cleaners, I worried about putting my wallet somewhere safe while I walked around frantically trying to organize the new house. I remembered my wallet and went out to retrieve it from the car. I saw the guy dressed in black in front of my house.

As I made my way to the car I noticed the gate to our backyard was open. It then occurred to me that the young man I saw the day before was homeless and had been living in our backyard the entire time the house stood vacant. I opened the car and my wallet was gone. He took it!

The Holy Spirit's small, quiet voice urged me, "Go talk to him. Go talk to him."

"I will not!" I thought loudly. I got in my car and left. The next day, I saw him again and I muttered, "That's right, just keep walking up the hill and return my wallet!"

After that, I didn't see him again and he didn't return my wallet. Three months later, Tim found my wallet in a drawer in the office. It was then that I felt the Lord put on my heart, "That was your Guardian Angel. I sent him to give you peace."

In the last encounter with my angel, I was trying to move my car from an icy parking lot. I was afraid to move it as the left front wheel slid into the car beside me. I needed help! As I glanced up, my eyes fell on a man who looked to be living out of his car. He looked at me and a wave of peace washed over me. Love exuded from him as he guided me out of the lot. As he calmly gave me instructions, I recalled the man in the black studded jacket. I knew the Lord was working to release pride from my mindset to teach me to receive what He has for me.

We often reject people as His blessings because we expect them to look or behave a certain way. Never underestimate the power of someone who looks different from you. It just might be your guardian angel.

~Maria Eansor

# Week 45

*"But the hour is coming, and is now here, when the true worshipers will worship the Father in spirit and truth, for the Father is seeking such people to worship Him." ~John 4:23*

## READING PLAN

| | |
|---|---|
| Day 1: | Luke 23-24 |
| Day 2: | John 1-3 |
| Day 3: | John 4-6 |
| Day 4: | John 7-9 |
| Day 5: | John 10-12 |
| Day 6: | John 13-15 |
| Day 7: | Rest Day/Catch Up |

## Faith in Action

Help someone in need. Pray for a stranger that God lays on your heart.

Week 45   Date: _____

# Journal Questions

1. John 3:14 mentions the serpent in the wilderness that Moses held up. How were the people in the wilderness healed? How does that relate to what John is saying about Jesus in this scripture?

2. John 12:43 says, "They loved the praise of men more than the praise of God." Are you guilty of this? Do you fall into the trap of worrying more about what man believes, and praises you for, than God? What shift will you make to improve this?

3. How can you stay in the "True Vine?" Reread what it says in John 15 and journal about it.

4. John talks about how men loved darkness more than the light because their deeds were evil. What does "darkness" represent? Is there any "darkness" in your life that you are harboring that God wants you to release?

## Week 45

### Reflection & Notes

### Gratitude

# Inspiration

This story may seem unbelievable, but God does the unbelievable right? He can work beyond what is humanly possible. I was 18 years old and in a disturbing relationship. (Story of my life!) One night, my boyfriend came to see me, and we got into a fight. He took off on his motorcycle. I quickly decided to chase after him and jumped into my car.

I remember very clearly hearing the voice of God repeatedly saying to my heart, and in my head, "Rachel, turn around, go back home. Don't chase him. Turn around, go back home, turn around, go back home." It was such a powerful force. I'll never forget it. I even stopped my car and looked back at home, almost turning around, but I was driven to find him and ignored that warning.

I took off down the road. Once I was off the gravel road, I reached the highway and quickly picked up speed trying to catch up to my boyfriend. As I pulled out from an intersection and onto a curvy main road, I picked up speed again. I remember going about 65 to 70 miles an hour, which was later confirmed when accident scene detectives measured the skid marks.

Suddenly, as fast as lightning, my car was swerving off the road and heading straight for a huge tree twice the size of my car.

In those couple of seconds, I knew I didn't have a seatbelt on, so I braced my arms straight against the steering wheel. I was driving a 1982 Toyota metal box and there were no airbags. I remember crashing into that tree and my whole front chest smashing into the metal steering column. It hurt, but I was numb. I lay there flung back in my seat and watched as, with each breath I took, blood bubbled out of my lungs and spilled onto my chest.

I remember feeling myself fading. I knew this was it. I could feel death approaching. I saw in my mind's eye my mother weeping that I was in Heaven, and I saw my feet separated, one on Planet Earth and one in Heaven. At that moment, I knew I was living a double life, and if I died it would be forever.

I prayed earnestly to God to spare my life and give me another chance. It's then that I saw a blue car pull up on the side of the road and a man, who I know was Jesus, walked up to me. I heard him say very clearly "Rachel, it is ok now, I am here now, I am here now. It is ok." I knew at that moment I would not die. Fear left, and I felt relief.

He walked over to me, bent down and put His hand through the broken glass window and touched my chest. The blood disappeared; my chest was healed. I remember looking in His eyes, and just seeing and feeling all of eternity and all of this love and the answer to life finally known. As He stood up and walked away, I stared in awe and watched, and then He did the most beautiful thing: He turned His face to look back at me and smiled.

I can never forget this. It was a miracle of God, but more than that, it taught me about God's love and mercy and, most importantly, eternity and happiness.

When I think about it today, I remember His smile, and I remind myself that God is love. He is always wanting to love and heal us. God is the answer to the human heart, the human condition, and the healing of our world.

~Rachel McCarter

# Week 46

"Repent and be baptized every one of you in the name of Jesus Christ for the forgiveness of your sins, and you will receive the gift of the Holy Spirit." ~Acts 2:38

## READING PLAN

| | |
|---:|---:|
| Day 1: | John 16-18 |
| Day 2: | John 19-21 |
| Day 3: | Acts 1-4 |
| Day 4: | Acts 5-7 |
| Day 5: | Acts 8-10 |
| Day 6: | Acts 11-14 |
| Day 7: | Rest Day/Catch Up |

## Faith in Action

Do something bold to share the love of Jesus with others this week.

Week 46            Date: _____

# Journal Questions

1. When the apostles received the promise of the Holy Spirit on Shavuot (pentecost), how many were saved that day? (Acts 2:41) Go back and read the account in Exodus 32:28 about the golden calf incident. How many died that day? Do you see any similarities?

2. Stephen was a bold apostle for Christ. Read his account of Jesus in Acts 7. Why was he killed? Did his death shock you?

3. What are some things you notice about the body of believers in Acts? What do you see that we could improve upon today as the body of Christ?

4. What are two ways you were challenged in the readings this week? Is there an area you can improve in your walk of faith as modeled by the apostles? What actions will you take?

# Week 46
# Reflection & Notes

# Gratitude

# Inspiration

My husband and I have always been Christian leaders. We helped out at church, led youth groups, directed worship, and tithed. Despite this, we struggled financially. Our income was cut in half because we had three children under five years of age and I essentially became a stay at home mom making a very minimal income from home.

Because we were barely hanging on by a financial thread, my husband and I resolved to drive cheap, old used cars that had a lot of miles on them and even more costly issues. I had just gotten my van back from the repair shop after a lengthy stay the previous day and wanted to take my kids out for the day.

We were stopped at a red light in a busy intersection when my engine shut off and I could not get it to turn over. I pumped the brakes and turned the key but to no avail. It was completely dead again.

My young son understood something was wrong and cried out in fear. His tears broke my heart and his fear spread to me as I surveyed my three babies in the backseat. "God please send someone to help me because I don't know what to do!" I whispered.

At that moment in the lane next to mine, I noticed a man looking at me from his car. As soon as the light turned green he pulled over to the side of the road and came over to help. He told me to pop the hood and I watched him put his head under it for less than a minute. He then told me he wanted to check something and walked around to the drivers side of my car and disappeared underneath it. He emerged within seconds, exclaiming happily, "I think I got it!"

As frustrated motorists honked their horns, angrily swerving around us, he reassured me we were okay and calmly asked me to turn the key one more time. My car started right up as if it were new. I was astonished and bewildered at how he knew to go to the side of my car, not to mention how he was able to fix it so quickly. I looked over to thank him and he smiled kindly and left.

This encounter helped me see that God truly sees us and He is taking care of us even when our lives appear overrun with trials. As I struggled with bills and wondered if God read the late notices stamped in big red squares, I realized He knows every hair on my head as well as every number in my accounting.

The angel He sent that day was loving, caring, and calm. He was just what I needed to trust in him so that I would allow him to help me. God didn't just send me an angel, He sent me one that was relatable and helped me lower my guard.

Before that encounter, I knew in my heart and mind to trust in the Lord for His provisions, but to see it in the flesh in real time during a trial was more assuring than mere knowledge in my mind. It was evidence that He would take care of me supernaturally even when I didn't know my next move. It proved to me that angels are watching over us, taking care of us, surrounding our house and protecting our families.

*~Sharon Marta*

*"And they were all filled with the Holy Spirit and began to speak in other tongues as the Spirit gave them utterance." ~Acts 2:4*

# Week 47

"Do not be conformed to this world, but be transformed by the renewal of your mind, that by testing you may discern what is the will of God, what is good and acceptable and perfect." ~Romans 2:12

## READING PLAN

| | |
|---|---|
| Day 1: | Acts 15-18 |
| Day 2: | Acts 19-21 |
| Day 3: | Acts 22-25 |
| Day 4: | Acts 26-28 |
| Day 5: | Romans 1-4 |
| Day 6: | Romans 5-8 |
| Day 7: | Rest Day/Catch Up |

## Faith in Action

Pray and ask God to reveal to you in what ways you are still walking in the flesh. Repent and turn back to His ways. Give Him praise for the ways in which He has helped you to walk according to His Spirit!

Week 47　　　　Date: _____

## *Journal Questions*

1. Paul talks about the constant battle of walking in the flesh versus the Spirit. What does it look like to walk in the flesh? What does it look like to walk in the Spirit?

2. Romans 8:1 tells us, "There is no condemnation for those who are In Christ." Are there areas where you still walk in condemnation instead of walking in Him?

3. Romans 8:31-39 is an incredible encouragement of God's heart for us. Read it over yourself several times and reflect on your response.

4. Paul defines the law as good and necessary. Without it (the law or Torah), we wouldn't know where we need to improve and that we are in desperate need of a Savior. Where did you "come from" that you needed Jesus as your Savior? How did you know you needed Him? What did He save you from?

# Week 47

## Reflection & Notes

## Gratitude

# Inspiration

On November 25th, 2021, my seventy-seven year old father was admitted to the hospital with covid pneumonia. He and my mother had both caught it and he went downhill very quickly. Five days later, he was intubated on a ventilator. On December 1st, the doctors told us he had one to seven days to live.

Family immediately flew in from all over. My husband watched the kids, and I spent my days at the hospital with my siblings.

A few days later, my 14 year old daughter, Jasna, asked me if she could come with me as I headed to my sister's house for the day. She was distraught and needed comfort. She had been with my parents when they got sick and was very close to them. I could tell she was shaken. I talked with her and prayed that the Holy Spirit would comfort her, give her peace, and let her know that He was with her.

A few minutes later, I received a text message that upset me so I decided to go home and rest. Jasna opted to stay at my sister's house, with everyone else.

Around 5pm, my siblings and Jasna were all praying together when suddenly, Jasna found herself in another room by herself. It was dark and there was a man standing in front of her. She didn't know who it was, but he spoke to her and said, "Everything is going to be okay."

She suddenly realized that it was Jesus in front of her! Just as suddenly, she was back in the room with everyone else. She began bawling and told them all what had happened.

A couple days later, we were told that my dad wouldn't make it more than a day. Days passed, and he was thankfully still alive.

December 26th, we got "the call" again to come and say goodbye. Ten of us went in and spent the day by his bedside praying. The doctor told us that he had irreparable brain damage, muscle wasting, and that his heart was starting to fail, and the compassionate thing to do would be to let him go.

My mom took several hours away to pray. She came back and decided to wait and see what happened.

The next day, a new doctor came in and examined my dad. He found nothing wrong with his heart!

My dad has since fully and completely recovered. He is able to take care of his own needs. He walks, talks, and has no sign of any brain damage! After 4 months in the hospital, he came home!

*"See, I am YHWH, the Elohim of all flesh. Is there any matter too hard for Me?"* Jeremiah 32:27

Not only did He heal my dad, but he comforted my daughter by showing up in-person to give her the message that everything would be okay. And He used this experience to strengthen our family in many ways.

*~Rachel Pops*

*"And we know that for those who love God all things work together for good, for those who are called according to his purpose." ~Romans 8:28*

# Week 48

*"Love is patient and kind; love does not envy or boast; it is not arrogant."* ~1 Corinthians 13:4

## READING PLAN

| | |
|---|---|
| Day 1: | Romans 9-12 |
| Day 2: | Romans 13-16 |
| Day 3: | 1 Corinthians 1-4 |
| Day 4: | 1 Corinthians 5-8 |
| Day 5: | 1 Corinthians 9-12 |
| Day 6: | 1 Corinthians 13-16 |
| Day 7: | Rest Day/Catch Up |

## Faith in Action

We live in a broken and fallen world and small acts of kindness can mean so much to others. Ask God how you can step up and show kindness to a stranger this week. Perhaps something as simple as buying the coffee of the person in line behind you at Starbucks and saying, "God bless you!"

Week 48    Date: _____

# *Journal Questions*

1. The Apostle Paul, brings a lot of correction and clarification about what it means to be a member of the Body of Messiah. There are many roles for many members. We get to embrace our individual role and gifts. What is your role in the body? What gifts do you bring?

2. Romans 11 talks about how the gentile nations were grafted into the olive tree. It's a powerful imagery given to us to show how God took us into His root and allowed us to be grafted in as if we were naturally born into the root. What does this "grafting in" look like? What does it mean for those "grafted in?"

3. Romans 12:12 says, "Do not conform to this world but be transformed by the renewing of your mind." How can you apply this to your life? Why is it important in your walk with God?

4. 1 Corinthians 13 is known as the "love" chapter. We know that God is love (1 John 4:26). For a different perpective try reading the chapter, replacing the word "love" with "God." How did doing this shift your perspective?

# Week 48
## Reflection & Notes

## Gratitude

# Inspiration

The Lord has healed me physically, spiritually, and emotionally many times, in many different ways.

I was a brand new Christian and had just been court-ordered to a Christian program. After being there for only a few days, we were playing volleyball at the church and I jumped up to hit the volleyball and heard a loud crack in my back. I fell to the ground in pain and I knew something had ruptured in my back.

At that time, I was on house arrest and was unable to go to the hospital without permission from my probation officer. It was a Saturday, so I was going to have to wait until Monday to get permission. That night I had a very hard time sleeping. It hurt to breathe, move, sit, and stand up. The next day at church, I told one of the ladies about it. She explained how she and two other ladies were going to pray a three-chord prayer over me for healing.

Honestly, I didn't really believe God would heal me because I was such a terrible person. The truth about grace, forgiveness and all that's available to us through salvation didn't really make sense to me yet.

The three ladies laid their hands on me. One of the ladies put her hand on the middle of my back where the pain was. As they began to pray, her hand started getting really hot. All of a sudden it was as if lightning shot from her hand through my back. I heard a bunch of cracking and popping and felt like there was fire in my back. When she was done, I was completely and totally healed! I was blown away. All I could say was, "Did you hear that? Oh my gosh, did you feel that your hand was on fire? My back was on fire!"

Those beautiful, mighty women smiled at me with a knowing smile and told me healing was part of my salvation. Jesus died so that I could be healed. His body was broken for me so that mine could be made whole. Since then, the Lord has healed me on many different occasions.

That day I discovered healing is real and healing is for now! Healing is for every born again believer, all daughters and sons of the living God. The Lord wants to heal us every single time we are in need. It is His will that we are healed. His Word says by His stripes we are healed. It does not say we were healed or we might be healed someday, but we are healed now! Psalm 103 says, *"Jesus heals all of our sicknesses and diseases and He forgives all our iniquities. He makes us whole."* Stand on His promises throughout the Word and see them manifest in your life. Step out in faith and be healed!

~Lynette Riganto

"Love is patient and kind; love does not envy or boast; it is not arrogant." ~1 Corinthians 13:4

# Week 49

*"I can do all things through Him who strengthens me."*
*~Philippians 4:13*

## READING PLAN

| | |
|---|---|
| Day 1: | 2 Corinthians 1-7 |
| Day 2: | 2 Corinthians 8-13 |
| Day 3: | Galatians 1-6 |
| Day 4: | Ephesians 1-6 |
| Day 5: | Philipians 1-4 |
| Day 6: | Colossians 1-4 |
| Day 7: | Rest Day/Catch Up |

## Faith in Action

Put on the full Armor of God. Read Ephesians 6:11-18 out loud every day this week.

Week 49      Date: _____

# *Journal Questions*

1. Paul had a "thorn in his side." (2 Corinthians 12) We are not told what the "thorn" is, but rather that it was some sort of hardship or pain, either physical or spiritual. Perhaps we are not told so that we are able to bring whatever hardship we are suffering in the place of this story. What hardship or struggles has God walked you through?

2. As believers, we are challenged to die to our flesh daily. Our flesh brings corruption, old patterns, and sin. What are the workings of the flesh mentioned in Galatians? What are the workings of the Spirit? What "flesh" do you still need to put to death? What workings of the Spirit can you pray for?

3. Read and meditate on Ephesians 2. It is your adoption story. You are adopted into the citizenship of spiritual Israel. What does that mean to you?

4. Compare the Armor of God (Ephesians 6: 11-18) to the Levitical priesthood garments (Exodus 28: 2-42). Some people think there is a correlation. What do you think?

# Week 49
# Reflection & Notes

## Gratitude

# Inspiration

I looked to my passenger seat for a split second to retrieve something from my purse and when I looked up traffic on the busy freeway had come to a complete stop in front of me. I heard my heart in my ears and felt the burn of adrenaline and fear as I slammed on my brakes. It wasn't soon enough to avert the fast moving impact. My Lexus collided into the car in front of me at fifty miles per hour. In turn, they hit the car in front of them and like dominoes the deafening crash continued to include five vehicles. My car was totaled.

I had hit the car in front of me so hard it caused my engine to drop out. I was told that if it had not dropped, five hundred pounds of steel and iron would have crushed its way inside the cabin of the car and caused such massive injuries that my legs would have been amputated. That was the first sign God was with me. Miraculously, I was able to get out of my car safely and make my way to the side of the freeway where a gentleman walked up and inquired how I was.

I assured him I was relatively intact but that my shins hurt from the impact of the engine hitting my legs. As I anxiously surveyed the accident scene, I assumed he was in the accident. With my guilty conscience I asked, "Which one are you?"

He assured me he was not a victim in the accident and explained that he was a doctor who had stopped to check on me. He asked again, "Are you sure you are okay?"

I looked at all the people climbing out of their cars. They seemed to tremble as they pulled themselves out, bracing on the side of their vehicles as if to steady their legs. They looked at each other in confusion, then back at their cars. One young woman was crying and an older gentleman gestured frantically as he spoke into his cell phone. I watched a woman circle her car examining the damages in detail before snapping pictures of it all. She got back into her driver's seat sideways, legs dangling out of the door and buried her face in her hands. I wondered about her story and how this wreck impacted these individuals in greater ways than just damage to their automobiles. I felt strangely removed from the scene and resolved myself to pray as soon as I was alone.

I turned back to answer the kind doctor and he was gone. His presence had been so comforting, warm, and reassuring, I scanned the crash scene hoping to find him, anticipating seeing him among the wrecks of other cars offering his medical assistance. He seemingly disappeared as quickly as he came upon the scene of the crash. Without a parting word, he had simply vanished.

As I stood taking inventory of the wreckage, coming to the horrific realization of what I had caused, I realized an angel stopped to calm me. This understanding felt palpable and assuring. I was guilty but not condemned. Standing on two hurt legs I had escaped disability and death. I was very much still there and I knew I was not alone in the wreck, but traveling in the company of angels.

~Lu Ann Topovski

# Week 50

"And may the Lord make you increase and abound in love for one another and for all, as we do for you." ~*1 Thessalonians 3:12*

## READING PLAN

| | |
|---|---|
| Day 1: | 1 Thessalonians 1-5 |
| Day 2: | 2 Thessalonians 1-3 |
| Day 3: | 1 Timothy 1-6 |
| Day 4: | 2 Timothy 1-4 |
| Day 5: | Titus 1-3. Philemon 1 |
| Day 6: | Hebrews 1-8 |
| Day 7: | Rest Day/Catch Up |

## Faith in Action

Pray and ask God to help your unbelief and show you blind spots in your faith so that you can be strengthened in your walk with Him.

Week 50     Date: _____

# *Journal Questions*

1. 1 Timothy 4:10 tells us to "fix our hope on the living God, who is the Savior of all the people, especially those who believe." How can you fix your hope in Him in this season of your life?

2. What does it look like to walk in a spirit of "power, love and a sound mind?" (2 Timothy 1:7)

3. What can be some goals you can have for yourself based on what is referenced in Titus 2?

4. What is something you had to let go of from your past to help you move forward as a believer and deepen your relationship with God?

# Week 50
## Reflection & Notes

## Gratitude

# Inspiration

I was twenty-six years old the first time I woke up with hands so red and swollen I could barely move them. Tying my toddlers' little shoes with wiggling feet was difficult. I had three small children under the age of seven to take care of. I didn't have time to think about my hands that morning. I got up and going as best I could. Sippy cups don't fill themselves and diapers have to be changed, no matter how clumsy you feel, with swollen, aching hands.

I thought that morning was a fluke. I wondered if I had slept on my hands in a strange position or eaten too much salt the day before, but the symptoms continued for months. The pain intensified every morning and began to spread to the rest of my body. Before long I was waking up with swollen hands, feet, ankles, and knees. Three months after the pain began, I could no longer squeeze the shampoo out of the container by myself, open a water bottle, tie my children's shoes or turn the key in my car's ignition.

When you're in your mid-twenties, it's hard to accept that anything might be seriously wrong, even when that's exactly what your body is clearly telling you. I knew I couldn't avoid it any longer and scheduled a visit with a specialist. My fears were confirmed when the doctor informed me that I had an incurable autoimmune disease called rheumatoid arthritis. It's difficult to explain the wave of emotions that come over you when you learn your body is attacking itself.

I spent six agonizing years trying to adapt to a perpetual state of physical, mental and emotional exhaustion. I struggled every day just to accomplish basic tasks. I dreamed of sleeping seven hours and waking up with enough energy and strength to put on makeup or fix my hair and feel like a "normal" woman. I wanted so desperately to take my babies to the park and push them on the swings without being totally wiped out. Simple activities like bike rides, jumping on the trampoline, or taking a day to go fishing required too much energy. Trying to do everyday family activities typically meant I'd spend the next three days in bed with a flare-up or end up with some kind of illness or infection.

After six years, I decided I'd had enough. I was angry about all the years I'd "missed" and I was determined not to miss any more. I knew God wanted more for me. My healing journey with God took time. It was fraught with trial and error as well as prayer and obedience. I had to learn to open my heart and mind to listen for the instructions Jehovah Rapha, the God who heals, gave me. Today I am completely healed. I have not had any symptoms nor medication for almost eleven years. My doctors said curing my disease was impossible. My God says all things are possible.

God is still a God of miracles. Sometimes healing happens instantly. Other times, as in my case, God invites us to partner with Him in our healing as He gives us specific instructions for our journey. Both forms of healing are miraculous. Accept the invitation from Jesus to embark on your own journey to healing and I believe there will be a radical breakthrough in your body, mind, and spirit. Jesus clearly tells us what He desires for us all in John 10:10: *"I came that they may have life and have it abundantly."*

~Dafne Wiswell

# Week 51

"But in your hearts honor Christ the Lord as holy, always being prepared to make a defense to anyone who asks you for a reason for the hope that is in you; yet do it with gentleness and respect."
~1 Peter 3:15

## READING PLAN

Day 1: Hebrews 9-13
Day 2: James 1-5
Day 3: 1 Peter 1-5
Day 4: 2 Peter 1-3
Day 5: 1 John 1-5
Day 6: 2 John 1, 3 John 1, Jude 1
Day 7: Rest Day/Catch Up

## Faith in Action

Take some time to self-reflect through the readings this week. Pray and seek God in areas you need to let go, things that need to not be a part of your walk, and things to add to your walk with Him.

Week 51    Date: _____

# Journal Questions

1. In Hebrews 11 we are given examples of stories of great faith. What stands out to you about the faith of these people? How is your faith today? In what ways have your hardships or trials in life grown your faith?

2. James talks about how our belief in Jesus leads us into good works. What are "good works" as defined in scripture?

3. There are consequences to sinning against God. What is sin? Look at 1 John 3:4. What is the difference between "sin" and "temptation?" Can they be the same? Why or why not?

4. The scriptures we read this week all seem to talk about the potential of "falling away." It's mentioned often, which makes it seem like a warning of relevance. According to this week's reading, what does "falling away" from faith or God look like? What can you do to keep that from happening to you?

# Week 51
## Reflection & Notes

## Gratitude

# Inspiration

My husband, Ivan, was a logger. His job was on the ground cutting down trees. The days started early for him. Before he left, I would pray with him for protection. We had been praying like that for a whole month. God had told me to do this with my husband in response to my question to Him, "How can I honor my husband." So I had been faithfully praying for his protection every morning before he left for work, declaring, "No weapon formed against him would prosper."

December 15, 2009, was not a typical day. Upon attempting to cut his second tree, my husband's chainsaw got stuck in the tree before he was finished cutting it. He quickly motioned the skidder operator for help. The skidder came and pushed the tree over. The vibration of the tree falling caused a large seventeen foot branch hung up in another nearby tree to come down like an arrow. The branch pierced Ivan in the head, breaking his hard hat into a million little pieces, and putting a golf ball sized hole in the top of his head. The intense pressure inside his head at that moment also caused his brain to break the bone behind his eye, pushing part of his brain into his eye socket. His boss, the skidder operator, saw it happen and ran over to him and declared, "In the name of Jesus, you will not die today!"

They were working down in a deep valley where there was no cell reception, but their 911 call was miraculously able to get out. When the ambulance and fire truck showed up they realized they would not be able to get him to a hospital in time to save his life, so they called for a helicopter. By the grace of God, a medical helicopter from Mayo Clinic was miraculously in the air almost right above them at that moment and dropped down to pick him up. Within seven minutes, they got him to a tiny little hospital that was not usually properly staffed with any doctor that would have been able to save him or give him proper care.

Thankfully, that day the top US Army doctor from Bethesda, Pennsylvania, happened to be doing a two week training there and immediately took charge of Ivan's surgery to save his life. He knew exactly what to do, as he had done surgeries of the same kind on countless wounded soldiers. Our pastor overheard him talking to the other doctors, standing his ground and telling them, "No, you are not doing it that way, you are doing it my way."

Ivan's life was miraculously saved that day. God had prepared for a miracle by pre-ordering all the little details in advance to bring about the exact care needed, at the precise time needed. In the moment of our greatest need, God was already there! He was in the hospital a total of sixteen days until he was able to walk again. He suffered paralysis on his right side. Much therapy was needed. In many aspects, he is still in recovery, but today he and I own and operate a cattle ranch running around 1400 animals. God is so good, preparing solutions to problems before they even exist.

~Marilyn Sadlier

"Count is all joy, my brothers, when you meet trials of carious kinds." ~James 1:2

# Week 52

"And they overcame him by the blood of the Lamb, and by the word of their testimony; and they loved not their lives unto death."
~Revelation 12:11

## READING PLAN

| | |
|---|---|
| Day 1: | Revelation 1-3 |
| Day 2: | Revelation 4-7 |
| Day 3: | Revelation 8-11 |
| Day 4: | Revelation 12-15 |
| Day 5: | Revelation 16-19 |
| Day 6: | Revelation 20-22 |
| Day 7: | Rest Day/Catch Up |

## Faith in Action

Pray this prayer: "Father, thank you for Your set apart Word that has filled me up and is alive and active. You are the Creator of all things and I thank you today for the ability that I have to sit and read Your Word every day. Thank you for giving me the strength and endurance to read Your entire Word. Praise You! All glory and esteem is Yours forever and ever. Amen!"

Week 52    Date: _____

# Journal Questions

1. Our testimony holds power. How do you define "testimony?" What is your testimony?

2. In Revelation 2-3, we find Jesus in the midst of the local church. The churches had their issues, but Jesus was still there. How are you doing in being a part of and serving in a local church family, or in your community?

3. Revelation is a book to help our hearts and minds prepare for the return of our Messiah. Are you prepared? How can you be more prepared and joyfully anticipating His return?

4. YOU DID IT! Now that you have finished, write out how you are feeling about accomplishing this goal of reading the Bible cover to cover!

# Week 52
## Reflection & Notes

## Gratitude

# Inspiration

God moves in miraculous ways. That was the conviction in our hearts when we moved from Vancouver in British-Columbia to pastor a small but vibrant congregation in Sherbrooke, Quebec. Six months into our new ministry appointment, the global pandemic struck. All public gatherings, including church services, were prohibited for several months. In the Fall of 2021, our government allowed churches to hold small worship gatherings with no more than 25 people. On a cold Sunday morning, a man with a cane walked into our intimate worship service and quietly sat among us. According to sanitary regulations we were at maximum capacity. Regardless, the greeter at the door had welcomed this stranger and allowed him to attend. That welcome would change his life forever.

Steve was a broken man who had experienced severe trauma. In his early twenties, he decided to become a priest. He joined a Catholic order and lived in a monastery. Because he was articulate and enthusiastic about the message of salvation, one of the nuns dubbed him "Stephen of the Gospel Proclamation." Unfortunately, once he completed his probationary stay at the monastery, he was told by his spiritual directors that monastic life wasn't for him.

He was disappointed and angry. Rather than seeking how to channel his faith in new ways, Steve rebelled against God. However, his recovery and his life remained unstable, marked by addiction relapses, money problems, sexual immorality, and spiritual emptiness.

He eventually made his way to northern Quebec where he hoped to have a fresh start. It is there he was lured by a colleague to a party that turned into a terrifying scene. He was savagely assaulted by a group of men and left for dead, naked in a snowbank. Steve should have died that night, but during the ordeal he cried out to God to deliver him. Steve eventually recovered from the assault, but was left with deep psychological and physical injuries.

A few months later, he walked into our church, now homeless, struggling with severe PTSD, a permanent hip injury and a limp, and chronic pain which he managed with a daily cocktail of medication. At the end of the church service, we asked him if he would like to receive prayer for his leg, assuring him we had witnessed other miraculous healings before. He accepted. We gathered a few believers around and laid hands on him. Our guest immediately felt the power of God at work. The chronic pain in his body left him and instantly he could walk perfectly straight. He was flabbergasted and so were the believers around him who had never or rarely witnessed an instantaneous healing. Afterwards, we bought him lunch, dropped him off at the local shelter, and arranged to meet again with him that week. Over the following weeks we learned his story, he gave his life to Jesus, we did inner healing prayer with him, and even took him out shopping for new clothes. That divine appointment, on a chilly Sunday morning, became a discipleship relationship.

Steve has since moved away, but we have remained in contact. With God's grace he weaned off the pain meds, has given up sexual immorality, and fought his way back from a drug relapse. He called us recently to plan a date for his water baptism. He insisted on doing it at the church that welcomed and accepted him, and dared to love him with prayers of faith, a meal, and lasting friendship. This was a miracle the pandemic couldn't stop.

~Caroline Duocher

# Walk In His Ways

Are you going to experience heaven for eternity with our Savior? If your answer is "yes," praise God!

If you're not sure, you *can* be sure. First - repent. You've now read His whole Word and you have a much better understanding of what He seeks in His children. You have fallen short. We all have. Repent of your sin. To repent means to turn away from sin and to turn to God. So turn today.

Repenting looks like: Asking for forgiveness. He's willing and ready to forgive you today. Just ask Him! "Father forgive me for..."

Now choose to walk in His ways, everyday. Ask Him to be Lord of your life and King in your heart. His answer will be "Yes!" Will you mess up again? Yep! Just repent, friend. Every time. Repent, and turn back.

There will be a time for every knee to know Him and bow. Choose Him. He's worthy. He's worth it.

# Celebrate! You Did It!

You completed reading the entire Bible cover to cover!

Take a picture with your Bible and give Him all the praise for this accomplishment.

Invite others to join you and start again. Everyday we get to choose Him and His Word.

Now that you have finished, we'd love to read what this journal and study has done for you! Email us at: *stories@StudyHisWord.com*.

# Prayer Log

| Date | Name | Prayer Request |
|------|------|----------------|
|      |      |                |
|      |      |                |
|      |      |                |
|      |      |                |
|      |      |                |
|      |      |                |
|      |      |                |
|      |      |                |
|      |      |                |
|      |      |                |
|      |      |                |
|      |      |                |
|      |      |                |
|      |      |                |
|      |      |                |

Copyright © 2022 Fear Into Faith Incorporated

# Prayer Log

| Date | Name | Prayer Request |
|---|---|---|
| | | |
| | | |
| | | |
| | | |
| | | |
| | | |
| | | |
| | | |
| | | |
| | | |
| | | |
| | | |
| | | |
| | | |
| | | |

Copyright © 2022 Fear Into Faith Incorporated

You can go to www.StudyHisWord.com to print more Prayer Log pages if you need them.

# Praise Report

| Date | Praise Report |
|------|---------------|
|      |               |
|      |               |
|      |               |
|      |               |
|      |               |
|      |               |
|      |               |
|      |               |
|      |               |
|      |               |
|      |               |
|      |               |
|      |               |
|      |               |
|      |               |

Copyright © 2022 Fear Into Faith Incorporated

# Praise Report

| Date | Praise Report |
|---|---|
| | |
| | |
| | |
| | |
| | |
| | |
| | |
| | |
| | |
| | |
| | |
| | |
| | |
| | |
| | |

# Notes

# NOTES

# Save the Date!

September 12-14, 2024

## End of the Year Celebration

We want to celebrate with you when you finish reading the Bible cover to cover. In 2024, we will celebrate with men and women on September 12-14th in Dallas, TX. At this event, we will get the opportunity to finish reading the last part of the book of Revelation together, which will be a POWERFUL moment you won't want to miss! We would love to have you there.

Visit **www.FearIntoFaithLIVE.com** for more info.

## Would you like to receive future books from Kingdom Mindset Publishing absolutely free?

We like to give away free copies of our books each month!

We could use your help.

God is calling us to create more Bible study guides in the near future. We would appreciate hearing your thoughts on this 52-Week Bible Study Guide. Your feedback will assist us in improving the next round of books with sections, guides, and resources you would like to see. We have put together a brief 2-minute survey.

To be entered into our monthly drawing, simply fill out the survey at:
www.StudyHisWord.com/survey

# More From Kingdom Mindset Publishing

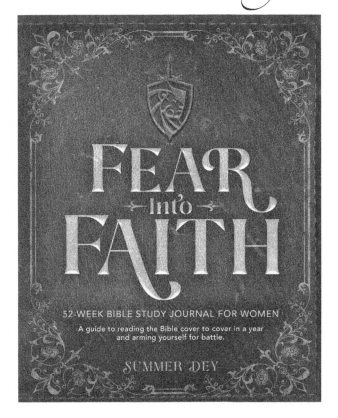
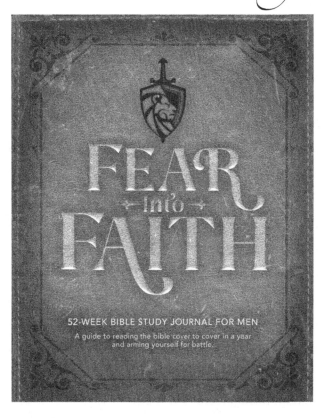

*"Finally, be strong in the Lord and in the strength of His might. Put on the whole armor of God, that you may be able to stand against the schemes of the devil." ~Ephesians 6:10-11*

There is no greater tool to arm God's people against the schemes of the Enemy than for them to be in the Word of God each and every day. We are excited to offer you the **Fear Into Faith: 52-Week Bible Study Journal for Women** and **Fear Into Faith: 52-Week Bible Study Journal for Men**, for those who want more tools to study His Word. It is time for us to be in His Word, to put on the armor of God each and every day, and to lead our families as God has called us to.

www.StudyHisWord.com

# Inspirational Stories

| | |
|---|---|
| ~Bishop Musisi Grivas . . . . . . . . . . . . 20 | ~Brandi Del Rio . . . . . . . . . . . . . . . . 124 |
| ~Jamie Gatchell . . . . . . . . . . . . . . . . 24 | ~Natasha Schuerman . . . . . . . . . . . . 128 |
| ~Mandrae Collins . . . . . . . . . . . . . . . 28 | ~Brit Coppa . . . . . . . . . . . . . . . . . . . 132 |
| ~Mark Thompson . . . . . . . . . . . . . . 32 | ~Maureen Brundage . . . . . . . . . . . . 136 |
| ~Stacy McLain . . . . . . . . . . . . . . . . . 36 | ~Jackie Dighans . . . . . . . . . . . . . . . 140 |
| ~Thomas Altemus . . . . . . . . . . . . . . 40 | ~Janice Gresser . . . . . . . . . . . . . . . . 144 |
| ~Devin Schubert . . . . . . . . . . . . . . . 44 | ~Timothy Curtis . . . . . . . . . . . . . . . 148 |
| ~Apostle Jessica Maldonado . . . . . . 48 | ~Mary DeAcetis . . . . . . . . . . . . . . . 152 |
| ~J Loren Norris . . . . . . . . . . . . . . . . 52 | ~Robert Henkleman . . . . . . . . . . . . 156 |
| ~Christine Baterbonia . . . . . . . . . . . 56 | ~Shannon Gort Eckhoff . . . . . . . . . 160 |
| ~Karissa Collins . . . . . . . . . . . . . . . . 60 | ~Chris Dorrity . . . . . . . . . . . . . . . . . 164 |
| ~Amber Pearl Anderson . . . . . . . . . 64 | ~Jenell Kelly . . . . . . . . . . . . . . . . . . 168 |
| ~Peter Nieves . . . . . . . . . . . . . . . . . . 68 | ~Nina Williams . . . . . . . . . . . . . . . . 172 |
| ~Ann C.K Nickell . . . . . . . . . . . . . . 72 | ~Allison Johnson . . . . . . . . . . . . . . . 176 |
| ~Crystal Jordan . . . . . . . . . . . . . . . . 76 | ~Nancy Johnson . . . . . . . . . . . . . . . 180 |
| ~Benjamin Foust . . . . . . . . . . . . . . . 80 | ~Maya Baker . . . . . . . . . . . . . . . . . . 184 |
| ~Michelle Rene' Hammer . . . . . . . . 84 | ~Rhonda Gordon . . . . . . . . . . . . . . 188 |
| ~Anne "Auntie Anne" Beiler . . . . . . 88 | ~Maria Eansor . . . . . . . . . . . . . . . . 192 |
| ~Ben Miller . . . . . . . . . . . . . . . . . . . 92 | ~Rachel McCarter . . . . . . . . . . . . . . 196 |
| ~Todd Sanford . . . . . . . . . . . . . . . . . 96 | ~Sharon Marta . . . . . . . . . . . . . . . . 200 |
| ~Summer Dey . . . . . . . . . . . . . . . . 100 | ~Rachel Pops . . . . . . . . . . . . . . . . . 204 |
| ~Raquel Foreman . . . . . . . . . . . . . 104 | ~Lynette Riganto . . . . . . . . . . . . . . 208 |
| ~Todd Jones . . . . . . . . . . . . . . . . . . 108 | ~Lu Ann Topovski . . . . . . . . . . . . . 212 |
| ~Erin Mansour . . . . . . . . . . . . . . . 112 | ~Dafne Wiswell . . . . . . . . . . . . . . . 216 |
| ~Dr. Charlie Fowler . . . . . . . . . . . . 116 | ~Marilyn Sadlier . . . . . . . . . . . . . . 220 |
| ~Jennifer Loza . . . . . . . . . . . . . . . . 120 | ~Caroline Duocher . . . . . . . . . . . . 224 |

# Before You Go!

We have a gift we would like to give to you!

We hope you have enjoyed your journey through the Bible cover to cover. We know the importance of not only studying His Word, but also the importance of memorizing scripture verses and having them in places where you will see them often.

We have created special Bible verse cards with the 52 verses found in each week of this journal. We would like to bless you with them.

Go to **www.StudyHisWord.com** to print off your free Bible verse cards.

You can put them up around your home, carry them in your wallet, give them as gifts, etc. We pray they will be a powerful reminder of the time you have spent in His Word and what His promises are to you.

"Let the word of Christ dwell in you richly, teaching and admonishing one another in all wisdom, singing psalms and hymns and spiritual songs, with thankfulness in your hearts to God." ~Colossians 3:16

## About the Journal Creator

SUMMER DEY is a Global Faith Influencer and International Speaker and Success Coach who helps people from around the globe shift FEAR into FAITH. She has spoken to, and motivated, thousands on platforms all over the world. She uses her voice and her influence to "set captives free" and to take back territories for the Kingdom.

She is the proud Proverbs 31 wife of Marcelo and a homeschooling mother of three beautiful warriors. In 2020, they sold all of their belongings to "pick up their mat and walk," and moved into an RV to travel around the country and serve wherever God calls them.

## Pastoral & Biblical Advisor

JEREMY ANTHONY is a charismatic, compassionate pastor with a desire to see people discover their destiny in Christ through teaching, discipleship, and the practical application of God's Word. Born in Minnesota, but raised in New Zealand, he has completed multiple degrees in computer science, Bible and missions. He has served as a youth pastor, church planter, lead pastor, and executive pastor. His passion for God's word comes from his father who was a pastor, missionary and bible school teacher. He and his incredible wife, Kariann, have three wonderful kids, all of whom are his priority and joy.

Made in the USA
Columbia, SC
01 September 2024